CHURCH AND HUMAN RIGHTS

JEAN-FRANÇOIS SIX

CHURCH
AND
HUMAN RIGHTS

 St Paul Publications

Original title: *Religion, Église et droits de l'homme*
© 1991 Desclée de Brouwer, Paris, France

Translated by Susan Leslie

Cover picture: 'Io uomo' by Franco Orlandini, Italy

Photo by Raymond Nicholls

St Paul Publications
Middlegreen, Slough SL3 6BT, United Kingdom
Moyglare Road, Maynooth, Co. Kildare, Ireland

English translation © St Paul Publications 1992

ISBN 085439 368 4

Printed by The Guernsey Press Co. Ltd, Guernsey, C.I.

St Paul Publications is an activity of the priests and brothers of
the Society of St Paul who proclaim the Gospel through the media
of social communication

Contents

Introduction:
The development of the
human rights

Christian concern with what are now recognized as human rights issues can be traced from the very beginnings of Christianity. However, it is basically since the Second World War that human rights have been a regular feature on the agenda of the Churches throughout the world. In terms of the Churches' practical involvement, violations of human rights have been denounced, causes espoused, and submissions made to individual governments, the United Nations and other responsible agencies. Attempts have also been made by individual theologians, Church commissions and ecumenical groups to formulate theological perspectives for the guidance of Christians who support human rights issues.

Origins – Historically, the origins of the concept of human rights can be traced to ancient Greece and Rome. It was closely linked to the pre-modern natural law doctrines of Greek Stoicism, whose founder, Zeno, taught that a universal working force pervades all creation and that human conduct therefore should not violate the law of nature. A classic example of this is for defying his command not to bury her slain brother, asserted that she acted in accordance with the immutable laws of the gods.

Roman law, which was influenced in its formation and spread by Hellenistic Stoicism, similarly recognised the existence of natural law and upheld certain universal rights that extended beyond the rights of citizenship. Thus the Roman jurist Ulpian expounded that natural law was that which nature – not the State – assures to all human beings.

However, it was only after the Middle Ages that natural law doctrines became closely associated with liberal political theories about natural rights. Till then the emphasis was on the duties rather than the rights deriving from natural law. As evident in the writing of Aristotle and St Thomas Aquinas, these natural law doctrines accepted the legitimacy of slavery and serfdom, thus excluding the concepts of freedom and equality which are the pivotal ideas of human rights as we understand them today.

Human rights had to wait for a long time to be recognized as a general social need. The changes in the beliefs and practices of society after the Middle Ages, and especially during the Renaissance, truly laid the foundations of what we now call human rights. There was increased resistance to religious intolerance and political-economic bondage. There was also disaffection with rulers who failed to meet their natural law obligations. And then there was the unprecedented commitment to individual expression and social experience that was characteristic of the Renaissance. These factors effected the shift from natural law as duties to natural law as rights. Proof of this change is found in the writings of Aquinas (1224-1274) and Hugo Grotius (1583-1645) on the European continent and in the *Magna Carta* (1215), the *Petition of Rights* (1628) and the *Bill of Rights* (1689) in England.

All reflected the increasingly popular view that human beings are endowed with eternal and inalienable rights, never lost in the passage from the primitive to the social state and never diminished by the claim of 'divine right of kings'.

The perception of natural law as implying natural rights was elaborated upon in the seventeenth and eighteenth centuries. The discoveries of Galileo and Newton, the materialism of Hobbes, the rationalism of Descartes and Leibniz, the pantheism of Spinoza, the empiricism of Bacon and Locke, promoted a belief in natural law and universal order. In the eighteenth century a growing confidence in human reason and in the perfectibility of human affairs led to a more comprehensive expression of natural rights.

Particularly significant in this context are the writings of the seventeenth century English philosopher, John Locke, and the works of the eighteenth century philosophers of Paris, including Montesquieu, Voltaire and Rousseau. Locke argued, mainly in his writings on the Revolution of 1688, that certain rights naturally pertain to individuals as human beings; that chief among them are the rights to life, liberty and property; that, upon entering civil society through a 'social contract', the citizen surrendered to the State only the right to enforce these natural rights, not the rights themselves.

The philosophers, following Locke and others and embracing diverse currents of thought with a common supreme faith in reason, vigorously attacked religious and scientific dogmatism, intolerance, censorship and social-economic restraints. The theory of the inalienable rights of the individual became their fundamental ethical and social gospel.

The Western world of the late eighteenth and early nineteenth centuries was greatly influenced by this liberal intellectual ferment. It brought on the wave of revolutionary agitation that swept the West, most notably in North America and France. Thomas Jefferson echoed Locke and Montesquieu in the Declaration of Independence by the thirteen American colonies on 4 July 1776: 'We hold these truths to be self-evident, that all men are created equal, that they are endowed by their Creator with certain inalienable rights, that among these are life, liberty and the pursuit of happiness.'

Similarly, the Marquis de Lafayette, who shared the hardships of the American War of Independence, stayed close to the declarations of the English and American revolutions in the *Declaration of the Rights of Man and of the Citizen* on 26 August 1789.

The declaration proclaims that men are born and remain free and equal in rights and that the aim of every political association is the preservation of the natural and imprescriptible rights of the individual, these rights being liberty, property, safety and resistance to oppression. The declaration includes, in the definition of liberty, the right to free speech, freedom of association, religious freedom and freedom from arbitrary arrest and confinement. We thus see that the idea of human rights played a key role in the struggles against the political absolutism of the late eighteenth and early nineteenth centuries.

Human rights as natural rights, however, had their opponents even in those liberating times. Philosophical and political liberals became less enthusiastic about natural rights which were being increasingly associated with religious orthodoxy. Natural rights also suffered from being conceived in absolutist terms which brought them into conflict with one another. Thus the doctrine of natural rights came under powerful philosophical and political attack.

The idea of human rights, nonetheless, endured as evidenced in the abolition of slavery, factory legislation, popular education, trade unionism, the universal suffrage movement. But it was with the rise and fall of Nazi Germany that human rights received due attention. The laws that authorized the dispossession and extermination of Jews and other minorities, the laws that permitted arbitrary police search and arrest, the laws that justified imprisonment, torture and execution without public trial and other such aberrations, showed conclusively that it is disastrous to base law and morality on purely utilitarian or idealist doctrines. Human beings have certain rights, irrespective of any circumstances.

In the second half of the twentieth century we have seen universal acceptance of human rights in principle and no government would want to be seen to dissent from this ideology. It can be fairly said that we have witnessed the birth of the international recognition of human rights. The founding treaty of the United Nations bound members to take joint and separate action for safeguarding human rights and fundamental freedoms for all without distinction of race, sex, language or religion. In 1948 representatives from diverse cultures endorsed the principles set forth in the Universal Declaration of Human Rights as a common standard of achievement for all peoples and all nations. And the year 1976 saw the coming into force and effect of the *International Covenant on Economic, Social and Cultural Rights* and the *International Covenant on Civil and Political Rights* which had both been approved by the the United Nations General Assembly in 1966.

Definition – Although the principle of human rights is accepted on the domestic and international planes, there is still no unanimous agreement about the nature and scope of such rights. Several questions have been raised. Are human rights divine, moral or legal entitlements? Are they validated by intuition, custom, social contract, distributive justice or are they prerequisites for happiness? Are they partially revocable or totally irrevocable? Such questions are likely to persist as long as there are scarcities of resources and differing approaches to public order.

Notwithstanding these questions, consensus seems to converge on the fact that human rights represent people's aspirations for shaping values in society, especially respect and tolerance. Power sharing, the creation of wealth and the promotion of enlightenment are among the chief priorities of such aspirations, which are bound to clash with those of persons and institutions that obstruct legitimate laws and traditions. The power of the State is limited by human rights, which are concerned with both the legal and the moral spheres.

When a right can be shown to be a human right it is to some extent the right of all human beings, sometimes even of the unborn. Unlike hereditary rights and other such privileges, human rights extend to all regardless of merit. However, in practice it is difficult to talk in absolutist terms about human rights as they are restricted by the comparable rights of others and the aggregate common interest. This factor has led some theorists to limit human rights to one or two fundamental rights such as the right to life and the right to equal freedom of opportunity. This brings us back to the controversial question of the content and legitimate scope of human rights.

The human rights tradition, like other traditions, is a product of its time. Its substance and form have been shaped by the processes of historical continuity and change. It may therefore be useful to note the dominant schools of thought and action that have influenced the human rights tradition in recent centuries.

The English, American and French revolutions reflected the aspirations generated by civil and political rights.

The emphasis was on the abstention rather than the intervention of government in the quest for human dignity. This is the chief aim of Articles 2-21 of the dignity. This is the chief aim of Articles 2-21 of the Universal Declaration of Human Rights, which include: freedom from racial and equivalent forms of discrimination; the right to life, liberty and the security of the person; freedom from slavery or involuntary servitude; freedom from torture and from cruel, inhuman or degrading treatment or punishment; freedom of movement and residence; the right to asylum from persecution; freedom of thought, conscience and religion; freedom of opinion and expression; freedom of peaceful assembly and association; and the right to participate in government, directly or through free elections. And two further rights fundamental to the interests fought for in the American and French revolutions and to the rise of capitalism, were the right to own property and the right not to be deprived of one's property arbitrarily.

Some of these rights cannot obviously be secured without a degree of positive government action rather than abstention. But the main thrust of these rights is the notion of liberty which acts as a shield against the abuse and misuse of political power. This particular idea of liberty is enshrined in almost every constitution of some 160 states today. It is seen as a triumph of the individual over the state.

The economic, social and cultural rights originated from the socialist tradition which first struck root in early nineteenth century France. It is a response to unbridled capitalist development which saw no wrong in the exploitation of working classes and colonial peoples. These rights, unlike civil and political rights, sought the intervention of the State as illustrated in Articles 22-27 of the Universal Declaration of Human Rights such as the right to social security; the right to work and protection against unemployment; the right to rest and leisure, including holidays with pay; the right to a standard of living adequate for the health and well-being of self and family; the right to education; and the artistic production. These rights which are essentially claims to social equality, have been slow in gaining international recognition. But with the phenomenon of a 'revolution of rising expectations' in the Third World, economic, social and cultural rights are beginning to be treated seriously.

Stemming from the rise and decline of the nation-states in the second half of the twentieth century are what are known as the solidarity rights. They were foreshadowed in Article 28 of the Universal Declaration of Human Rights, which states that everyone is entitled to a social and international order in which human rights can be realized. There seem to be six such claimed rights. Three of these are linked to the emergence of nationalism in developing countries and the demand for a global redistribution of power, wealth and other important values – the right to political, economic, social and cultural self-determination; and the right to participate in and benefit from the common heritage of humanity. The other three solidarity rights – the right to peace, the right to a healthy and balanced environment, and the right to humanitarian disaster relief – reflect the inadequacy of the nation-state in crucial areas of need. The majority of these rights, however, tend to be more aspirational rather than practicable.

Thus the content of human rights has been broadly defined at various stages of modern history. The definition is shaped by the evolving perceptions of which values need special attention at which periods. To that extent, the history of the content of human rights is also a record of our aspirations for change and continuity.

There is no guarantee that the above three categories of rights are equally acceptable to all. Those who advocate civil and political rights tend to exclude the second and third group from their definition of human rights. What they see as aspirational and vaguely asserted claims to entitlement fail to qualify as proper rights in their canon. The most cogent argument, however, is more ideological than political in nature. Proponents of civil and political rights take the view that collective egalitarian claims against the rich erode liberty and the quality of life as they invite State intervention for the redistribution of wealth. They therefore favour the view that human rights are independent of civil society.

Defenders of the other two categories of human rights instead believe that civil and political rights are insufficiently sensitive to material human needs and are sometimes at the service of unjust social orders. They are seen as long-term goals that will be achieved only with fundamental economic and social transformations.

We are thus led to conclude that different conceptions of rights, especially new ones, can challenge the legitimacy of one another and of the political and social systems with which they are closely associated. This in turn could lead to sharp disagreements about the proper scope of human rights and their priorities. The debate is useful only insofar as liberty and individualism are shown to be used as excuses for the abuses of capitalism or equality and collectivism as alibis for authoritarian rule. But it could also make us lose sight of essential truths necessary for an objective understanding of today's worldwide human rights movement.

One-sided emphasis of legitimacy and priority of any set of human rights only serves to put in doubt the political credibility of their proponents and the worth of their particularistic values. Today groups and societies are more interdependent than in the past, and any human rights ideal that does not aim for the widest possible shaping and sharing of values is unlikely to get general support.

Another useful point to note is that one-sided characterization of legitimacy and priority does not necessarily correspond to human aspirations. In reality ordinary people insist upon the equitable production and distribution of all basic values.

In the literature of international human rights agencies there is no mention of legitimacy or rank-ordering of the rights they are trying to promote. Disagreements about legitimacy and hierarchy of claimed rights only arise when lawyers, moralists and political scientists have to deal with the question of implementation. But, as the UN General Assembly has repeatedly stated, all human rights form an indivisible whole.

The United Nations and human rights – The Charter of the United Nations (1945) reaffirms 'faith in fundamental human rights, in the dignity and worth of the human person, in the equal rights of men and women and of nations large and small.' The purposes of the United Nations are, among other things, 'to develop friendly relations among nations based on respect for the principle of equal rights and self-determination of peoples... and to achieve international cooperation in promoting and encouraging respect for human rights and for fundamental freedoms for all without distinction as to race, sex, language or religion.'

On the basis of individual petitions, statements from witnesses, state complaints, and reports from non-governmental organizations, the United Nations has investigated and evaluated specific human rights situations. The United Nations has also not hesitated to recommend or prescribe concrete action in certain cases. The imposition by the Security Council in 1977 of a mandatory arms embargo against South Africa is a case in point. No doubt, UN bodies set up for the promotion of human rights suffer from most of the same handicaps that affect the United Nations as a whole. Power politics and the absence of supranational authority often make it difficult for the United Nations to act swiftly and effectively. Nevertheless, where there is a political will the UN organs for promoting human rights usually succeed.

The UN's central policy organ in the human rights field is the inter-governmental body called the Commission on Human Rights, which operates under the Economic and Social Council which in turn derives its authority from the General Assembly. The commission's work is mostly investigatory, evaluative and advisory in character. Violations of human rights are referred to it by its Sub-commission on Prevention of Discrimination and Protection of Minorities. Every year the commission establishes a working group to study and make recommendations concerning these cases. Special representatives and envoys are also appointed by the commission to study particular human rights problems.

Together with other UN bodies such as the International Labour Organization, the United Nations Educational, Scientific and Cultural Organization (UNESCO) and the UN Commission on the Status of Women, the Commission on Human Rights has prepared a number of international human rights instruments. The most important of these are the *Universal Declaration of Human Rights* (1948), the *International Covenant on Civil and Political Rights* (1976), and the *International Covenant on Economic, Social and Cultural Rights* (1976). These three instruments, collectively known as the International Bill of Rights, serve as yardsticks for interpreting the human rights provisions of the United Nations Charter.

The Universal Declaration of Human Rights was adopted by the General Assembly on 10 December 1948. It includes all the important political and civil rights of national constitutions and legal systems. Not being a treaty, the declaration sets a common standard of achievement for all peoples rather than enforceable legal obligations. Nevertheless, the status it has acquired over the years is juridically more important than originally intended and has been used, even by national courts, for judging cases involving violation of human rights.

The International Covenant on Civil and Political Rights and the Optional Protocol, which came into force in 1976, incorporates almost all the civil and political rights proclaimed in the Universal Declaration. In accordance with the covenant, each State party undertakes to respect and to ensure to all persons within its territory and subject to its jurisdiction the rights recognized in the covenant. Some rights listed in the Universal Declaration such as the right to own property and the right to asylum are not included in the covenant. But it does designate a number of rights not listed in the Universal Declaration, among them the right of all peoples to self-determination and the right of ethnic, religious, or linguistic groups to foster their culture, religion and language.

A complement to the International Covenant on Civil and Political Rights is the International Covenant on Economic, Social and Cultural Rights. It elaborates on most of the economic, social and cultural rights proclaimed by the Universal Declaration. This covenant, however, is not on the whole structured for immediate implementation. It can be described as a promotional convention which stipulates objectives rather than standards and requires eventual rather than immediate results. There is, however, one obligation which is subject to immediate application: the prohibition of discrimination in the enjoyment of rights enumerated on grounds of race, colour, sex, language, religion, political or other opinion; national or social origin; property and birth or other status.

Besides the covenants mentioned above there are numerous other human rights treaties framed and adopted under the auspices of the United Nations. They refer to a broad range of concerns: the prevention and refer to a broad range of concerns: the prevention and punishment of the crime of genocide; the humane treatment of military and civilian personnel in time of war; the status of refugees; the protection of stateless persons; the abolition of slavery, forced labour and discrimination in employment and occupation; the elimination of all forms of racial discrimination; the fight against discrimination in education; the promotion of the political rights of women and the elimination of all forms of discrimination against women; the promotion of equality of opportunity and treatment of migrant workers. Many of these treaties are the work of the UN specialized agencies, and many also provide for supervisory and enforcement mechanisms.

Other international agencies – Outside the United Nations, concern for human rights has been most notably evident in the Conference on Security and Cooperation in Europe, convened in Helsinki on 3 July 1973 and concluded on 1 August 1975. Attended by representatives of 35 governments including the NATO countries, the Warsaw Pact members, and 13 neutral and non-aligned European states, the main concern of the conference was the definition of peace and stability between East and West, which was not possible before due to the Cold War.

The Soviet Union was concerned with the recognition of its western frontiers as established at the end of the Second World War. But having no realistic territorial claims of their own, the Western powers pressed for certain concessions in respect of human rights and freedom of movement and information between East and West. Thus the participating governments declared their determination to respect and put into practice, alongside other guiding principles, respect for human rights and fundamental freedoms, including the freedom of thought, conscience, religion or belief and self-determination. This was indeed to mark the beginning of the liberalization of authoritarian regimes in Eastern Europe.

The Helsinki Final Act adopted by the conference was not intended as a legally binding instrument and there were no provisions for enforcement machinery. However, the Declaration of Principles Guiding Relations Between States subscribed by the participants has always been accepted as consistent with international law. The Final Act's human rights provisions have indeed served as important guiding norms in dealing with perceived violations. Thus the Helsinki Final Act, though not a treaty, has created widespread expectations and facilitated the monitoring of human rights policy.

In Europe, the Americas, Africa and the Middle East, action for the international promotion and protection of human rights has proceeded at the regional level. In the first three zones there are now enforcement mechanisms within the framework of a human rights charter.

The most advanced and successful international experiment in the field is the European Convention for the Protection of Human Rights and Fundamental Freedoms, which came into force on 3 September 1953. A similar instrument is the European Social Charter (1961). The charter has an elaborate system of control through reports to the various committees and organs of the Council of Europe. The effective instruments created under the European Convention are the European Commission of Human Rights and the European Court of Human Rights. They have developed a considerable body of case law on questions regulated by the convention.

In 1959 a consultative meeting of the American Ministers for Foreign Affairs created, within the framework of the Organization of American States (1948), the Inter-American Commission on Human Rights. It has since carried out important investigations concerning human rights in the Americas. Ten years later, the Inter-American Specialized Conference on Human Rights, meeting in San José, Costa Rica, adopted the American Convention on Human Rights. Its substantive law and procedural arrangements are markedly influenced by the UN covenants, the European Convention and the European Social Charter. Under the American conventions, the right of petition by individuals, groups and non-governmental organizations operates automatically.

Following numerous pleas from the UN Commission on Human Rights, interested states, non-governmental organizations, and others, the Eighteenth Assembly of Heads of State and Government of the Organization of African Unity convened in Nairobi, Kenya, in 1981 adopted the African Charter on Human and Peoples' Rights. The charter makes provisions for both promotional and protective functions. There are no restrictions on who may file a complaint. The charter does not envisage a human rights court. African customs and traditions favour mediation and conciliation rather than adjudicative procedures.

It is noteworthy that the African charter provides for economic, social and cultural rights as well as civil and political rights. In contrast to both the American and European conventions, it recognizes the rights of groups like the aged and the infirm besides the family, women and children. The charter is also unique in claiming as belonging to all peoples the right to economic, social and cultural development and the right to national and international peace and security. The African charter is so far the only treaty instrument to detail individual duties as well as individual rights.

How have international human rights fared in domestic courts? Using domestic courts to redress violations of international human rights is still a relatively new approach. There are the inevitable interpretative problems of applying conventional norms that are fashioned in multi-cultural settings. Controversial theories about the inter-relation of national and international law as well as many procedural difficulties complicate the invoking of human rights norms in domestic courts. But recent decisions handed down in various domestic courts constitute evidence that considerable progress is being made in this area.

The Church and human rights – Although human rights have often been perceived as a secular phenomenon by the Churches, theological insights have played an important role in defining the nature of human rights and responsibilities. The concept of human dignity in the Judaeo-Christian tradition stresses that human beings are made in the image of God. In this tradition God is portrayed as treating men and women with respect. Therefore every human being is also to be shown respect by others. The mystery of sin has not obliterated the image of God from human beings. Hence they still possess much dignity.

The life and death of Jesus Christ are a sign that God has an overall plan for humanity. Human beings are therefore to be honoured and treated as sacred. But human life is flawed. From the Christian point of view, the need to affirm human rights arises because of human sin. Human rights are a means of controlling the exercise of power which in human hands easily tends to corrupt.

But, paradoxically the Churches have also neglected human rights. In the nineteenth century, the Roman Catholic Church rejected the liberal concept of human rights on the grounds that the individual was being elevated at the risk of undermining social order and the common good. The popes saw in the demand for freedom of expression and religious liberty the threat of relativism and the erosion of absolute values. While individual theologians and thinkers continued to argue for a decisive commitment to human rights, it was mainly at the Second Vatican Council that a specific Roman Catholic contribution to human rights was formulated. The teaching of the Church on fundamental human rights is rooted in the inherent requirements of human nature itself on the level of reason and within the sphere of natural law.

In the Incarnation of Christ the Church sees a reaffirmation of the dignity of human beings. Through his life, death and resurrection Jesus is seen to have sanctified all human beings, directing them to the love of neighbour. The Church perceives itself as the continuation of the presence of Christ in the world. Since the mission of Christ is redemption through liberation, the task of the Church is also to work for the liberation of humanity.

There still is no adequate explanation why human rights have not been affirmed by the Church throughout history, or why specific human rights only become apparent at certain times in its history. But a strong stress on human sin and on the eschatological nature of the Church as journeying towards the truth – themes that are recurrent in the Second Vatican Council and in the encyclicals of Pope John Paul II – has helped to highlight the specificity of human rights as safeguards against the use of power which violates human dignity.

In the wake of the Second Vatican Council and subsequent theological affirmation of human rights, movements have emerged in the Roman Catholic Church appealing for a bill of rights within the Church because some manifestations of Church authority are recognized as oppressive. This appeal is a clear reminder that the Church needs to take seriously all human rights values as a sign of God's care for every human being.

Alongside the Roman Catholic Church, other Christian denominations have also been active in the area of human rights. Through an examination of the Scriptures, the World Alliance of Reformed Churches came to conclusions similar to recent Roman Catholic studies, albeit placing greater emphasis on the liberating power of Jesus Christ. The Lutheran World Federation has instead stressed that human rights point to human sin, and that human rights are to be based in the three rights of freedom, equality and participation, which are analogous to the values of the Kingdom of God. Following these perceptions, the World Council of Churches has initiated an ecumenical study which explores the concept of power from a theological perspective.

It has, however, become even more obvious that the major problem with regard to human rights is not their enunciation but their implementation. The Churches are now active seeking to protect people from destructive uses of power and are promoting the development of human values, thus affirming that 'in Christ there is neither Jew nor Greek, neither male nor female' (St Paul's Letter to the Galatians 3:28).

Conclusion – It can be stated quite objectively that the demands for human rights across the world is a fact which no government or institution can ignore. The promotion of human rights has become a characteristic feature of contemporary world affairs.

The main bodies responsible for such change and progress are, of course, the United Nations and its allied agencies, the Council of Europe, the Organization of American States and the Organization of African Unity. Other factors that have helped are the public advocacy of human rights as an important ingredient of national foreign policies, first made legitimate by the example of U.S. President Jimmy Carter; the proliferation of activist non-governmental human rights organizations like Amnesty International, the International Commission of Jurists, and various Church-affiliated groups; and a worldwide growth in the study of human rights both in formal and informal educational settings.

At the same time, we cannot be blind to the formidable obstacles that have to be surmounted by human rights policymakers and activists. For the most part, the implementation of international human rights law is dependent on the voluntary consent of states. The agencies and mechanisms for the observance or enforcement of human rights are still in their infancy. But it is beyond doubt that the concern for the advancement of human rights will prevail as much out of necessity as out of idealism.

The Publishers

Preface

— It seems you have been asked to write a small book on the Church and human rights. Don't you find that a great deal has already been written on the subject?

— Yes, there are some weighty tomes, detailed, erudite and often controversial. Some say – I'm exaggerating, of course, – 'the Church is human rights!' Others, taking the opposite view, maintain that 'the Church has long opposed and condemned human rights; today it is no longer able to resist the surge of worldwide concern for those rights, so it makes the best of it, jumps on the band wagon, and turns things to its own advantage; the Church has made an about-turn on the subject of human rights and now embraces what it once condemned.'

— Well, that's a pretty fair general outline of what I feel myself, with certain nuances, of course. We could discuss it.

— That's how I want to write this book, in dialogue form. In dialogue with you and also with all those who don't share the Christian faith, with thinkers and historians of every persuasion. Also in dialogue with myself; I find this question extremely complex and I experience it as such in my own mind.

— Shouldn't you be writing a substantia book, setting down all the available data; something really solid, that can't be distorted, almost irrefutable, giving all possible viewpoints and showing what is, in the last analysis, the truth of the whole matter?

– That would be one solution. But, as I said, there are several books of that sort; I must admit that none of them convinced me and I found carefully-hidden assumptions in them all; that is only to be expected in books of that kind and it's all for the good; but I have no wish to proceed along these lines; I have a profound respect for such studies, but for the moment anyway, I have no desire to follow suit.

– What do you want to do, then?

– First, I have been asked to write a 'small book': so I haven't the space to develop my theme at length; I recommend to those serious-minded folk who wish to study the question in depth to read those weighty tomes; to the rest, folk like you, I propose a mere discussion of the problem, the simple sharing of a few modest ideas, so that together we can form some sort of opinion on the subject. I don't know if you've read about this: a few years ago, there was a philosopher in Holland who started a philosophy practice as one would start a medical practice; he gives consultations, listens to his clients and philosophises with them about life and death and the meaning of existence. He's a great success. He wisely remarks, 'You need more than a diploma for this job. You need to have experienced doubt and sorrow, in a word, you need to have lived a bit.'

– Too true; there are learned folk with all sorts of degrees who discourse on human rights; but sometimes one can't see exactly when they ever fought in a practical way for such rights except by signing a petition here and there. What you really want is to go half way, or rather to combine both approaches to the problem: especially in the last ten years, you yourself have put up a constant fight in various ways, one of them being through the activities of the Human Rights and Solidarity Movement; and you also make a continual effort to reflect on human rights: witness the white paper of the National Consultative Commission on Human Rights, of which you have been a member for ten years, too: that white paper was entitled Human Rights in Question Form, published in 1989 by the French Information Service of which you were co-ordinator.

– Yes, I would like to have a short, live exchange backed by both action and reflection, simple, dealing with essentials, not covering everything but bringing out the main points. Do you agree to this method?

– It seems a good way of doing it. Let's get going!

The genealogy of human rights

– Where do you want to start?

– At the beginning. Some people maintain that the Church initiated human rights, which I rather doubt; but what is the truth of the matter?

– One must always be careful, in this matter of human rights, not to make dogmatic statements and take all the credit. I feel like saying that human rights don't belong to anyone and that they did not originate with one particular individual or group of people but with humanity. Human rights are like a fruit that is the product of a long maturing process in which water, soil and sunshine have all played their part; millions of people have worked tenaciously so that, little by little, human beings might rise above the level of the animals and respect each other's rights. So human rights did not spring, one fine day, from the mind of some benevolent thinker who cried 'Eureka!'; they are the result of constant effort, the outcome of the cries of distress and the struggles of countless human beings: those sufferers from injustice, oppression, violence and exclusion, who resisted their oppressors and protested in defence of their rights, the right to exist, to live with justice and dignity.

And, with the invention of writing, codes of law were engraved in stone; this law took on a universal character in time and space, being valid for all: 'When laws are written down, both the rich and the weak obtain justice.' That is a verse from Euripides.

– There are laws, certainly, but also the interpretation of laws.

– Yes, there is a constant tension between the law and the spirit of the law, and also between written and unwritten laws. Antigone appeals in favour of the unwritten law against the written; she claims that there is a justice, an equity, superior to the written law, by which the written law may be interpreted. Greek philosophers will maintain that there is such a thing as human nature: something common to all human beings, which overrules all local customs and provides a point of reference for all peoples and all legal systems. Every human being shares the human nature, so every person represents all humanity; so from then on human beings are equal and these philosophers, at this early date, denounce slavery.

IF YOU TREAT HUMAN BEINGS AS HUMAN BEINGS

Unity between human beings is not just a word nor is it the logical outcome of some abstract argument. It is the living communion of individuals in the mystery of the human race; it is not confined to the realm of ideas but it is to be found in individual, concrete examples... Inasmuch as you treat human beings as human beings, that is, insofar as you respect and love the secret of their being and their capacity for good, approaching them as individuals, so you begin to realise their proximity and the unity of their nature with yours.

Jacques Maritain, 'Human Equality'
Works, Desclée de Brouwer, p. 1243

– So the Church was not the first to condemn slavery?

– Let us respect the historical facts. The idea of 'natural law' may be found in Socrates, Plato and Aristotle; this idea will be the foundation on which subsequent theories of human rights will gradually be constructed. The Stoics will think in terms of the 'universe': they feel they are part of a great cosmos and for them natural law extends to all living beings the world over; they declare themselves to be citizens of the world rather than of any particular nation; they also condemn slavery; in their eyes, slaves belong to the human community; human beings are unique simply by virtue of being human: as Seneca said, 'To humankind, humanity is sacred.'

The Old and New Testaments:
Humanity according to Revelation

– But what about the Hebrews at that period, and the
Bible?

– Before speaking of the Bible, we must look at
other texts of the Near East – and also some very
ancient Asian texts – which develop the theme of laws
and their purpose. In the code of Hammurabi – thirteenth century BC – the legislator states that these laws
have been laid down 'so that the strong should not
oppress the weak'. But already in the year 2000 BC an
important Egyptian official presents himself before the
gods in this prayer of self-justification:

> I was a man who cared for those in trouble,
> who buried the dead,
> who gave to the destitute;
> a man who was generous;
> he saved those in distress,
> he was a father to the orphan,
> he cared for widows.
> No one under my jurisdiction
> went hungry to bed.

– The poor and the oppressed are also given an important place in the Bible.

– Of course. And we should note this particular characteristic: in the Bible, it is God who reveals himself as the most constant and firm defender of the defenceless, the one who 'gives justice to the widow and orphan, who loves the stranger, giving him food and clothing' (Deuteronomy 10:18). 'God rises up to do justice, to save all the poor of the earth', says Psalm 87; and Psalm 146 describes God as he who cares for the most deprived: the oppressed, the hungry, the prisoners, the blind, etc.

And legislation in Israel is designed to assist God; it enables him to protect the poor and marginalised; those in authority, the government, have to respect this legislation; and when a king, for example, abuses his power by crushing the weak, a prophet appears to remind him of God's law and of how God expects people to live; the prophet is the one who sees with sorrow the disparity between what God has prescribed and what people actually do; he shouts, he denounces evil. So Adam – this is the generic term for a human being in Hebrew – must believe God, being like him and bearing witness to him, the one who defends the needy.

– But there's a bit of everything in the Bible, many tales of violence, for example. There are some things which are disconcerting from the point of view of human rights.

– The Bible is not an edifying document, a series of lives of saints. It shows how we should try to respond to the demands of God in the very heart of the human condition, in real flesh-and-blood situations; it doesn't provide ready-made prescriptions but it does pose the question of human rights. Right from the very beginning of the Bible; the most ancient creation story, in Genesis chapter 2, is an account which speaks of human beings and their way of life in this world; the editor of this passage affirms that God created humankind to enjoy fullness of life. It was after centuries of conflict with the divinities to which humankind felt obliged to submit – Fertility, Power, the Stars – that a second creation account was composed, the one we find at the beginning of Genesis, which speaks of humanity's primordial place among all living creatures. Human beings, every one of them, have a right to live; and they also have rights over the rest of creation.

– In the Bible it seems to me that human beings are those who are able to enter into dialogue with God, to listen to him and speak to him, without loss of dignity, standing upright before him. That is a manifestly optimistic vision of humanity. What about the Gospel of Jesus?

– Right from the start, the Gospel message is meant to be universal and cannot bear fruit unless it is proclaimed to beings who are themselves open to the universal; the radical invitation to practise the Beatitudes presupposes that every human being is able to receive and respond to this message; all human beings are equally able to do this and the God of the Gospel has no favourites.

– What is the significance of Jesus' death in this context? It is the death of an innocent man who has been condemned with a total disregard for human rights.

– The Christian faith shows, in the resurrection of Jesus, how God rises up against injustice and manifests himself as the God of the living, the one who will not allow people to deny a person's rights. I've always been struck by the fact that the resurrection of Jesus is in radical opposition to the argument of Caiaphas: 'It is better for one man to die for the people than the whole nation should perish' (John 11:50); it was on that day that the Pharisees decided to kill Jesus, arguing that the collectivity is of absolute value and it matters little if an innocent man is sacrificed. The resurrection of Jesus, on the contrary, emphasizes the primacy, individuality and inviolable nature of each person.

– According to the Christian view, God appears as the one who is firmly on the side of the oppressed; for him, a future promise of a 'supreme good' to be achieved can in no way justify the sacrifice of human beings to a cause. Christians, like those who conducted the Inquisition, did not respect such a God; for them, the 'supreme good' – in their eyes, the Catholic faith – demanded the elimination of those of other persuasions, who thereby tainted their ideology.

– You are quite right. The God of the Gospel does not crush those who do not believe in him; he makes his sun shine on those who believe in heaven and on those who do not believe, without distinction. He gives human beings the absolute right to be unbelievers.

– That is something which is important to me: has a human being, as such, any rights before God, and eventually even against him? There was talk of Jesus' trial. Officially, Jesus is condemned to death, deserves death because he has blasphemed against God. And here we also have a people defending themselves: to strike a blow at the faith seems to them to place Israel in danger, to jeopardize their national unity.

– In the same way, others will sentence to death those who attack the totalitarian ideology which 'unites' the majority of the people. The twentieth century is full of such condemnations, all over the world.

– Yes, that is a deplorable fact of modern life, but this modern death penalty for political blasphemy in no way justifies the Jewish condemnation for religious blasphemy. What is more, the Bible too often presents us with a vengeful God who crushes his enemies; they have hardly the right to exist in his presence.

– I'm going to go further than you. A whole school of Catholic theology has represented the death of Christ as just reparation for the outrage sinful humanity has inflicted on God; this theology adopts the position of Caiaphas: it is a very good thing for one innocent man to die on behalf of all sinful humanity. The God of the Gospel has nothing to do with this shameful exchange in which Jesus is an innocent hostage who will purely and simply be eliminated so that good relations may be re-established between God and his people.

– Let's go back a bit. In the Bible there is the figure of Job. In order to test him, it is said, God arranges that his wife and immediate family should abandon him,

---

INSPIRED BY THE GOSPEL

The proclamation of human rights in America and France at the end of the eighteenth century, when the peoples were urged to embrace the ideals of Liberty, Equality and Fraternity, represents a great act of defiance on the part of the common people; it is a proclamation made in a spirit of childlike faith, giving expression to an ideal of universal generosity, challenging the very heart of politics, with its powerful and worldly leaders, for the most part confirmed sceptics. The evangelical element which came to the fore in this way bear the marks of secularized Christianity; rationalist philosophy has made its contribution here, declaring that mere natural goodness and reason suffice to fulfil the great promise of justice and peace; illusions of this kind will soon lead to bloodshed.

But in the midst of these illusions a sacred truth becomes apparent, at least to some: it is indeed necessary that the influence of the Gospel be felt in the temporal affairs of humanity. The Good News which leads to heaven and eternal life must also be applied to the transformation of worldly societies with all their misery and conflicts. The Gospel mes-

---

that he become a public laughing-stock and lose all his dignity; even his children die.

Even if in the end God gives him more children, the first children are still dead and beyond recall. How can one posit a God like that? And Job, who believes in and persistently proclaims his own innocence, always returns to the fundamental question: why does this God permit the undeserved suffering of the righteous and the scandalous triumph of the wicked? Finally in the Book of Job, God, in a flood of eloquence in which he

---

sage has political and social implications which must at all costs be applied to history.

Often unwittingly, the secular conscience has responded to this powerful Gospel message and has understood the dignity of the human person. It has understood that individuals, gifted as they are with a mysterious but inalienable liberty of spirit and called as they are to unlimited happiness, are part of the state and at the same time transcend the state. The purpose of the state is to help people acquire the good things which make up a truly human life. If the secular conscience is not to lead to inhuman behaviour, it must acquire the Gospel faith in the rights of the human person as a member of the human race, as a citizen, as a person involved in social and economic life and in the work force. It is a faith in justice as the necessary foundation of community life and as the essential characteristic of the law, which is not law if it is unjust. The thirst for justice was introduced into the Christian era by the Gospel and the Church; it is through the Gospel and the Church that we learned not to obey a law unless it was just.

Jacques Maritain, 'Gospel inspiration and the secular conscience', *Christianity and Democracy*, Desclée de Brouwer, 1989, pp. 49, 50, 53

displays the marvels of creation, manages to (or attempts to) 'shut him up' (I can find no other way of expressing it) and Job submits and then has his honour, family and possession restored to him; dazzled by so many wonders of the divine intelligence, Job says to himself that God must have the answer to his question. But the Bible, in fact, does not give this answer; God keeps his secret, the answer is not forthcoming.

– The answer will come several centuries later with the belief in the resurrection. In the books of the Maccabees (about 100 BC). Job relies on his own integrity in order to make his case against God; in the very end, God casts no doubt at all on the innocence of Job and when God parades the wonder of his creation before him, it is not in order to crush him beneath these splendours and render him speechless, but to tell him that he, a human being, has been placed beside God. Job had framed the question in terms of rights; God replies in terms of reciprocal responsibility. God has entrusted to humankind the task of an overseer who must constantly watch over all living beings, a steward who must ensure that all human beings have real access to liberty, justice and peace. God has not created a complete but an incomplete world; and each human being must freely work out his or her destiny in time, with all the risks inherent in any enterprise. No one can take our place in this adventure of life; we each of us have to take full possession of our own liberty as we fulfil our task. But we are responsible for making sure that others enjoy conditions of true justice and peace in which to live their lives. Every human being has these rights.

– For you, the risen Christ is in fact the only person who is complete and absolutely whole.

– Yes, that is my faith. Which means that from now on every human being has the right to share in the resurrection of Christ.

– What does that mean exactly?

– The New Testament texts are clear on that point, especially the Johannine writings. Eternal life begins already here below; those who really love their brothers and sisters, who grant them the right to exist as much as or even more than themselves, those persons are truly alive; those who say they love God and do not love their neighbour are the living dead; it is not those who say 'Lord, Lord!' who are in a living relationship with God but those who respect and actively promote human rights according to God's will.

Roman law, natural law
and the Church in the Middle Ages

– I would like to go back to the original question about the Church and human rights. Or rather to continue the genealogy we began, the family tree of human rights.

– We had got as far as the Stoics. Roman law will take up the ideas of Greek philosophy and Stoicism. Cicero in his legal defence, *Pro Milone*, will speak of an 'unwritten law which is innate, being learned not from other human beings but from our very nature'; and in the *Republic* he will refer in the same way to natural law:

'There is a true law which consists of right reason in conformity with nature, common to all beings, always consistent, not subject to decay... No amendment to this law is permissible; it is not lawful to repeal it either in part or in its totality. This law does not differ from Rome to Athens; it is not one thing today and something else tomorrow. It is one and the same law, eternal and unchangeable, which guides all nations at all times.'

– Did this Roman law make its mark on the first Christians?

– Yes, unquestionably. St Irenaeus, the great theologian, speaks of natural law. Roman law will not cease to exercise its influence; it has a considerable influence on

Thomas Aquinas – there are numerous quotations from Roman law in his writings. One thing we must make clear: when this Christian theology speaks of 'nature', it means both those ethical demands in accord with God's plan as creator of humankind and the principle of all human activity, that which gives dignity and freedom to human beings, a point on which St Thomas is most insistent.

– At the same time, I imagine the Roman jurists continued to elaborate their own ideas.

– With some very interesting contributions to the gradual formation of the notion of 'human rights'. Gaius, for example, a second century jurist, makes an important distinction between 'civil law' and 'the law of nations': 'Every people governed by a written law and customs follows, on the one hand, a law which is peculiar to them and, on the other, a law which they share with the whole human race. The law which each people has made for itself and which is proper to it, is called civil law, the law belonging to the city. The law of natural reason common to all peoples is observed in the same way everywhere and is called the "law of nations".' Gaius recognises a law which is common to the whole of humankind.

– We are still far from a precise statement of human rights.

– This will be achieved in successive stages. We often hear quoted the great Charter of 1215, drawn up in France at the Abbey of Pontigny by English barons in revolt against their sovereign, King John; this is a document containing sixty-three articles, called *Magna Carta Libertatum* which seeks to put an end to royal abuses, particularly in the matter of taxation, by fixing the rights and duties of all. The Charter is accepted by King John, thanks to the intervention of the Archbishop of Canterbury. It is a compromise which seeks to reconcile contradictory claims: to grant privileges to vassals without affecting the unity of the kingdom and the absolute power of the sovereign. In fact the Charter serves to moderate the power of the monarchy and means that the king and his people are both subject to the law which must be the same for all. Individual rights and liberties are mentioned – article 39 outrules all arbitrary arrests; article 42 guarantees freedom of movement within and outside the kingdom and safeguards the rights of various social groups; article 61, for example, appears to establish a real right to rise in revolt: the sovereign who has violated his subjects' rights should be brought to reason by an uprising of the people, led by the barons. The great Charter in fact reinforces feudalism, but many of its articles lay the foundation for future human rights.

– The Church hardly contributed to this development, did it?

– In one way, we could say that during the High Middle Ages, the Church, along with the people of that time, tends to represent the *status quo*; but sometimes it too easily sides with this non-egalitarian society which it accepts as a consequence of human malice, the result of original sin. And the Church theorizes about the situation, saying that there are two sorts of law: fundamental natural law and secondary natural law; the first expresses the ideal, operative before the Fall, something which cannot be achieved except in the eschatological future; this is what the monastic life aims at, a sort of sanctuary outside the world which foreshadows that future time when fundamental law will have full sway; the second corresponds to real life with its everyday violence, injustice and oppression, the result of human malice, about which little can be done. The Church has been all too ready to accept this situation, and for centuries. Nevertheless, on a practical level, the Church has also worked continually to protect people from the excesses of war and to establish institutions to care for the sick and needy.

The Renaissance and the awakening of the Church in response to the discovery of the New World

– When did the Church begin to wake up?

– Even if the Church was all too easily satisfied with human equality simply on the level of the soul, it nonetheless never ceased to proclaim the ideal; and the message of human equality has always been among its teachings.

– But when exactly did the Church really begin to tackle the problem of human rights?

– Modern historians have shown how at the Renaissance there was a great revival of a theological trend which had its origins in mediaeval canon law and in Thomism. This revival was promoted by the particular problems arising from new scientific discoveries and from the discovery of the New World. And historians have proved conclusively that there is a definite relationship between these Renaissance theologians and the philosophers and jurists who were to formulate the declarations of human rights of the eighteenth century.

– So it would be interesting to take a look at the work of those Renaissance theologians.

– Yes. They are mostly Spaniards of the theological school of Salamanca. They hear of what is happening in the course of the colonial conquests and of the exploitation of the Red Indians. Bartolomé de las Casas, a Dominican, born in Seville and stationed in Haiti, is converted as he is preparing his Pentecost sermon in 1514: he suddenly realises that 'the treatment of the Indians is unjust and tyrannical'. He comes to Spain in 1519 and in a public debate brilliantly expounds the thesis of the Indians' natural right to freedom. We find him again in Nicaragua where he preaches against military conquests. He returns to Spain in 1539 and collaborates with theologians like the Dominican Franciscan de Vitoria who, in his teaching on the Indians, appeals to the 'law of nations' which recognises the Indians' right not to be enslaved or placed under protectorates, and their right to private ownership and to their own rulers. In his short work on the subject, Vitoria specifies certain human rights: the right to associate and communicate with others, the right to travel; and he develops a code for the treatment of aliens: the right to be treated humanely, the right to work and acquire property, the right not to be deported without just cause. It is Vitoria who lays the foundations of international law – he speaks of the 'natural laws proper to states': the rights of existence, integrity, defence and development (with the duty to help less fortunate states). After Vitoria, the Jesuit Suarez will develop the concept of international law (the great jurist Hugo Grotius will take up many of Suarez's ideas). Moreover, Suarez, at the beginning of the seventeenth century, does not hesitate to oppose the principle of the divine right of kings; he believes that political power should be in the hands of the people and that the state is based on a social contract to which the people give their consent; among other things, this leads him to conclude that the Indian territories are sovereign states, on an equal footing with Spain, and members of the world community; neither pope nor emperor has the right to conquer them or occupy them under the pretext of bringing them the Christian faith. At the same time we should note how Suarez destroys the old framework of mediaeval Christendom in which Christians were a privileged class: henceforward non-Christians are recognised as having the same rights as Christians. Suarez is a revolutionary figure.

– One can see why there is a quotation from Suarez above the entrance to the United Nations building in Geneva!

– Just now I mentioned Grotius. He is a Dutch Protestant and a great humanist. Along with other Dutch jurists, he carries on the work of the School of Salamanca and creates what is known as the School of Natural Law; these jurists no longer think of law and political harmony as coming from God or the divine right of kings but from reason and human nature. This school gives rise to the universalist philosophy whose principal exponents, in France, will be the Encyclopaedists and Jean-Jacques Rousseau. It is this philosophy which will take shape in the Declaration of the Rights of Man in 1789.

The English and human rights

– We must not forget England and what is happening there in the seventeenth century.

– In 1629 the House of Lords and the House of Commons make the king sign the *Petition of Rights* which limits the absolute power of the monarch, and outlaws arbitrary arrest and discrimination in matters of justice. In 1679 the *Habeas Corpus* act is passed: everyone arrested must be brought before a tribunal which is to judge of the legitimacy of the arrest; everyone may have the defence counsel of their choice.

In 1689 the *Bill of Rights* was passed, a declaration of the rights of the king's subjects. It should be noted that these rights were not granted all at once; they were the outcome of popular demands and insurrections: the revolution of 1649 against Charles I (who lost his head in the process), the revolution of 1688 against James II; they were not simply the result of principles worked out by some assembly of jurists in a council chamber; not a few of those jurists were subjected to inquisition and imprisonment.

The *Bill of Rights*, a century before 1789, marks a more precise definition of the rights and liberties of the citizen; however, there is no question here of such rights being founded on values and principles of a universal nature; they are particular rights, those of English citizens – not yet universal human rights.

– Yet there is the English philosopher John Locke, still in the seventeenth century, a philosopher concerned above all with practical politics; a true Englishman...

– Yes, he also starts from the principle of natural law and refers to universal human nature; therefore every human being has intrinsic rights which society or the sovereign should respect and promote. Locke's political theory will be the basis of the Declaration of the Rights of Man as such in 1776: the *Virginia Bill of Rights* which will appear again in the American Declaration of Independence on 4 July 1776. Locke is frequently quoted word for word in it; one could say that Locke, who published a *Letter on Tolerance* in 1689, just a century before the French Revolution, and who had a profound influence on Voltaire – ('I went back to Locke', he says at the end of his life when recalling his spiritual odyssey, 'as the prodigal son returns to his father') – was the 'father' of the earliest declarations of human rights.

The Americans

– What are the essential points of the American Declaration?

– Three points, above all. First that certain rights are inherent in human nature and are inalienable even by contract: human beings cannot totally transfer their rights to a superior authority representing 'the general will' (which is what Jean-Jacques Rousseau held). Then there is the insistence on private property considered as an inviolable natural right: bourgeois individualism was one of the historical sources of the tradition of human rights; we should also note the insistence on 'happiness' which is to be 'sought' and 'attained'.

Lastly, and this is of particular interest to us here, God is clearly and unashamedly mentioned; these inalienable rights are directly related to the divine plan.

– It was psalm-singing Protestants who set off, Bible in hand, for the New World, to establish a new society; they were deeply religious; so their faith shines forth strongly in the first Declaration of human rights.

– We have to be very careful here; these men and women are going to bring their Christian values to the young American nation; but, and this is not sufficiently appreciated, they are also going to bring the model of their own Church; if the Roman Catholic Church is marked by a hierarchical structure and a vertical form of government (often questioned from within its ranks, by Francis of Assisi for example, who in the thirteenth century insists on *fraternitas*, but always taken anew and re-imposed), the Churches of the Reformation, modelling themselves on the New Testament, set up very different ecclesiastical structures, based on mutual agreement and association. And in Pennsylvania the Quaker movement led by William Penn (1644-1718) rose up very early in defence of the principles of equality and religious freedom. That is why in the eyes of Rome, in 1776, human rights seem at first like a product of Protestantism and therefore a danger to the Catholic Church.

— Do you think it really made a difference?

— Yes, in a way, human rights, for Rome, are something of 'non-Catholic' origin. And so there arises a deep suspicion about human rights. Then the French Revolution will come to confirm Rome's view that human rights are aimed against the Catholic Church; soon some will be saying that the Freemasons and Protestants are plotting together against the Catholic Church.

— We haven't yet spoken of Freemasonry.

— It was on 24 June 1717 that the London Grand Lodge was founded; Masonry then developed rapidly in Great Britain and spread quickly to France and America. There was an astonishing growth of Freemasonry in the eighteenth century.

— The Catholic Church was suspicious of that, too.

— Yes, the Church sees the influence of the Reformation there, too; and she immediately reacts by condemning the movement in 1738, without much effect; there are many churchmen in the lodges in the century preceding 1789. Many 'revolutionaries', Mirabeau and Camille Desmoulins for example, were Masons. But above all we should stress the influence of the Masonic movement on the intellectual revival of the Enlightenment.

The Enlightenment

– One often hears of the age – or the philosophy – of the Enlightenment.

– This century – the eighteenth – is in fact marked by an intense desire to elucidate the whole of human reality in a systematic manner. It is a search for rationality on every front. The ideology of the Enlightenment abolishes all distinctions of rank: each individual is classified simply as a member of the human race. From the middle of the eighteenth century a certain number of philosopher-monarchs such as Frederick II of Prussia and Catherine II of Russia will be inspired by this ideology. Montesquieu's *The Spirit of Laws* (1748) and the Discourses of Jean-Jacques Rousseau (1750) represent a veritable explosion of conscience; they are in the mainstream of the Enlightenment; in the eighteenth century Freemasonry stresses this basic theme of an enlightened conscience; this ideology makes a strong impression on eighteenth century Europe.

– 'How can we better the lot of humanity?' asks Condorcet. 'By what means?' 'There is only one way', he answers: 'By speeding up the progress of the Enlightenment.'

– For the thinkers of the eighteenth century, it is a

question of discovering the truth. And they take up the old motto of the Reformation: *Post tenebras lux*, 'after darkness, light'. However, they never cease to insist on the full autonomy of the human spirit which should not submit to anything but the evidence of the senses. The Enlightenment is therefore in conflict with all forms of oppression – political, religious, intellectual – a real fight for the truth. It is also an ideology of hope: someone like Condorcet expresses his confidence in the unlimited perfectibility of the human race; he and his fellow philosophers await the dawn of a new era in which society will be humane, happy, just and peaceful.

– But there is Rousseau, too.

– The century of enlightened reason is also the great century of the novel, the century of sensitivity. That is where Rousseau comes in; nor should we forget that he was affected by the pietism which emerged in the eighteenth century alongside rationalism.

– Jean-Jacques Rousseau was familiar with Locke and the rationalist school of natural law. Both his fervour and his lucid style are to exercise an important influence in preparing people for the Declaration of Rights.

– In fact Rousseau takes up the idea of human nature which, for him, is essentially good: 'Human beings are born good; it is society that corrupts them.' The primitive state of humankind, the state of nature, is a time of goodness and innocence; it is a question of combatting the influences which have distorted human nature. What is the remedy for the corruption of society? Above all, a state where each person listens to the voice of conscience, where each individual is a citizen and makes a positive decision to be a responsible member of society: 'We each whole-heartedly place our own person under the supreme direction of the general will; and we accept and recognise each member as an indivisible part of the whole.' It is *The Social Contract* and the works of Jean-Jacques Rousseau, more than the American Declaration, which form the basis of the Declaration of the Rights of Man and of the Citizen of 26 August 1789.

– It's still a question of natural law. But is it the same concept, now in Rousseau, as in the Middle Ages?

– In fact, from now on there will be two ways of speaking of natural law. The Christian view of nature was built up, as we have seen, after Aristotle and the Stoics, on a metaphysical framework which is based on God as First Cause. Gradually, this Christian view gives way to another, quite different view; here we need to show how this came about, for example through the influence of a master of the school of natural law, Samuel von Pufendorf (1632-1694); this son of a Lutheran pastor, counsellor to the king of Sweden, who writes at the end of the seventeenth century, is an important source of inspiration for the American Constitution of 1787, published exactly a century after the book in which Pufendorf sets out its conception of the ideal relationship between Church and State. Pufendorf lays great stress on the contract established between persons of good will, if I can put it that way; that is, rational people who meet together freely and form what Pufendorf calls a 'general friendship' based on 'conformity to the same nature'. God starts to be excluded. If the Protestant strove to obey God alone and wanted no intermediary – either saint or priest – between his conscience and God, the *Age of the Enlightenment* wants to obey conscience and reason alone. Rousseau declares that moral conscience is innate: when we are presented with good and evil, we recognize them at once, loving one and hating the other, and it is this 'feeling' which is 'innate'. It is Robespierre in his *The Spirit of Laws* who refashions the judicial concept of law based on the model of the natural sciences.

1789: The Church and the Declaration of the Rights of Man and Citizen

– I'm impatient to get to the Declaration of the Rights of Man and Citizen of 1789.

– In the famous 1789 'lists of grievances' we can already find the idea of this Declaration. And when a 'Constitution Committee' is formed, precisely to compose the text of the new constitution, the committee proposes that the first work of the Constituent Assembly should be a 'Declaration of the natural and inalienable rights of man'. The committee, however, is divided on the subject of human rights; some of them, especially the representatives of the clergy, ask that alongside the Declaration of rights, there should be a Declaration of duties, in order to maintain public order; others oppose this, maintaining that duty is engraved in the human heart; the predominant group wished to show that natural rights had been disregarded for too long and that it was vital to acquaint the people with their own rights. And in fact all the articles of the 26 August Declaration are concerned with rights.

– The Declaration is published three weeks after the

night of 4 August in which all privileges were abolished and the modern state came to birth, with its concepts of the sovereignty of the people and equal rights for all. Each of the rights in some way sets out to counteract some abuses of the Old Regime.

– Yes, the 'lists of grievances' had done their work; they had drawn attention to these abuses and the injustices of a non-free society; it is this experience which led to the Declaration of Rights made to the people. In a way one could say that the continual abuses of the eighteenth century and the absence of any will to reform, more particularly in France than in other European countries, gave rise to such a vehement Declaration of rights. And this strong reaction can be seen in the profusion of proposed texts for the Declaration, more than twenty, which came out in July-August 1789 before the definitive text of the Declaration as we know it.

– So this famous text of 26 August 1789 is both a radical critique of the Old Regime and its sovereign, and the foundation of a new political regime, the state ruled by law. And what is important is the universalism of this text: the brief and lucid formulae are addressed to each individual and to all humanity and not only to the people of France.

– In the preamble there is a memorable sentence: 'The National Assembly recognises and declares, in the presence and under the auspices of the Supreme Being, the following rights of man and citizen.' Where does this idea of the Supreme Being come from? From Voltaire and Rousseau who, in the face of the Catholic intolerance which classed them as atheists, wished to introduce a purely philosophical and moral cult of the Supreme Being. We know that Robespierre, a disciple of Rousseau, having on the one hand branded atheism as 'aristocratic' and on the other rejected the clergy as unnecessary mediators with the divine, went on to impose a feast of the 'Supreme Being': 'The idea of a Supreme Being', he says, 'continually recalls us to a sense of justice and is therefore proper to a Republican society.' In this curious feast, celebrated throughout France, a hymn was sung to the 'Supreme Intelligence, father of the universe'. The eighth and last verse ran:

Free us from error, make us good and just;
Reign, boundless in might beyond all finite spheres,
Rivet our nature to your august decrees,
Leave to humankind their liberty!

– Meanwhile, the Church condemned the principles of the Declaration of the Rights of Man and Citizen.

– We must place these facts in their context. The Church will not condemn the Declaration at once. Less than a year after the Declaration, on 12 July 1790, a decree called the Civil Constitution of the Clergy will be passed; first of all, the Constituent Assembly wants to simplify things at an administrative level: the departments replace the complicated regions of the Old Regime; the members of the Assembly feel that it is best to create one diocese per department and one parish per commune, each member of the clergy receiving a suitable salary (1,200 francs a year for a parish priest, ten times that for a bishop). Taking things to their logical conclusion, the Assembly believes that the clergy should be elected by popular vote. Those who drew up this Constitution, it must be remembered, were good Catholics, fervent adherents of the Church, with a strong evangelical sense; they saw that the Church in France was far from perfect and wanted to renew it by abolishing abuses. In our eyes, certainly, they went beyond their mandate: it is not for politicians to meddle in religious affairs and seek to bring about reform. But, at that time, those elected were well acquainted with the 'lists of grievances' in which both clergy and laity demanded the thorough-going reform of ecclesiastical institutions; so they wished to respond to these appeals; and for the majority of the population, religion was the affair of the state and not just a private matter. The Assembly had to take action in the religious domain; it even represented the Church in France and told itself that it was going to succeed in bringing about the necessary reforms where Rome had failed to do so.

JOHN PAUL II SPEAKS ON THE DECLARATION OF THE RIGHTS OF MAN

This year we are celebrating the fortieth anniversary of the Universal Declaration of the Rights of Man. Although it is open to various interpretations, the lofty principles it contains deserve universal attention.

We consider the Declaration all the more important because it transcends the racial, cultural and institutional differences of the nations and passes beyond all frontiers to affirm the dignity of all members of the human community, a dignity which every society, national and international, should respect, protect and promote.

John Paul II, *To the Diplomatic Corps*,
9 January 1988

– Was that enough to make Rome condemn the Declaration of the Rights of Man and Citizen of 26 August 1789?

– In fact, the article in the text of the Declaration which had been the most debated, three days before, was article 10: 'No one is to be troubled on account of his opinions, even religious ones, as long as their expression does not endanger public order as established by law.' Which means in the end that the State should not favour any one religion, that it should be neutral. The Church will take up this position very clearly but not until the end of Vatican II, on 7 December 1965, in the Declaration on Religious Freedom. In 1789, no one envisaged this kind of separation of Church and State; on the contrary, everyone wanted them to be closely united. In fact article 10 was a declaration of tolerance to non-Catholics. But this article meant that Catholicism could not be known as the 'national religion'.

– And was it this that led to Rome's condemnation?

– Yes, the Church reacted first of all against it, as Pope Pius VI says in March 1791: 'The National Assembly has refused to declare Catholicism to be the main religion of the kingdom although it has always enjoyed this position until now.' But the Church's main objection to the 1789 Declaration centres on the problem of freedom; how, asks Pius VI, did they come to establish 'as a human right in society, this complete freedom which not only guarantees non-interference with religious opinions but also allows a person to think, say, write and even print anything about religion, however disordered the imagination of the author; a monstrous right which the Assembly however believes to be a result of the equality and natural liberty of all humankind.' Pius VI can come to only one conclusion: he fears that 'this legality, this liberty so vaunted by the National Assembly will serve only to overthrow the Catholic religion.'

– Is that true?

– Cardinal Lustiger maintains that at the time of the Revolution 'there was a deliberate attempt at de-christianization' but the historian François Furet corrects this impression by showing that the Revolution 'came into conflict with the Church without really wishing to do so... The revolutionaries did not deliberately set out to eradicate Christianity, apart from the de-christianization measures of the autumn of 1793.' Throughout this discussion (in the magazine *Debate*, no. 55, May-June 1989), Furet reminds us that 'the classical doctrine of 1789, more or less adopted by all democracies, is that religious belief is a private and personal matter, and that citizenship does not depend on one's religious denomination'; and the historian clearly shows that the Revolution conceives human rights 'in such a way as to affirm that society is the result of human will' whereas the Church 'thinks of human rights as being part of human nature as created by God.' Furet then introduces 'the problem of the compatibility between the Church and modern democracies': 'The Church is a monarchical structure which moreover has been both the matrix and the rival of European monarchies. In the last analysis, is the Church compatible with the world of democratic citizenship?' And he asks whether today 'the Church itself is not affected *from within* by democratic pressures.'

– One could ask why the American Declaration did not provoke a similar opposition on the part of the Church.

– Rome certainly realised that the 1789 Declaration was intended to be universal, transcending particular customs and periods of history and that it was therefore in direct and complete agreement with Catholicism which considers and presents itself as the religion of universal and eternal Truth. So we have two 'systems' of universal dimensions confronting each other and preparing to fight. But at the same time there is a very important and fundamental ideological incompatibility. Here is the National Assembly presenting people with absolute human rights, since everyone has the right to say what they like on the subject of religion; thus the Declaration rejects the idea of Revelation, even if it places itself 'under the auspices of the Supreme Being'. Those who take to themselves absolute rights in this way are setting themselves in opposition to God, claiming an independent existence, refusing to admit that they are creatures of God and sinners, whereas the doctrine of Christian salvation presupposes God as first point of reference, and teaches that we have duties to him; in 1789 Abbé Grégoire himself asked that human rights might not be proclaimed without at the same time affirming human duties, particularly to God.

– Joseph de Maistre, in his book on the pope, expresses the reaction of the Church in a short formula: '1789', he says, 'substitutes the reason and will of the individual for the reason and will of God'.

– The American Constitution, for its part, recognizes complete freedom with regard not only to personal convictions but also to institutional groups: adherents of any faith, Christian or otherwise, may organise themselves as they wish. It is the end of state religion as such, with the state representing one predominant faith.

– The French revolution and French law are more marked by Roman law and its rigidity than Anglo-Saxon law. But it is important to note in the American text that there is at the same time an insistence on 'God' as a general conviction and the relativisation of religions; the Catholic Church opposed this liberalism and relativism fairly strongly.

– At the end of the eighteenth century, the United States has to deal with a whole lot of people of different origins who have to be welded into a nation; at the same period, France is a nation, long since unified, which seeks to refashion itself, to build itself afresh on new foundations; she has become aware of the injustice and corruption in her midst and seeks renewal; there is a hint of sacred redemption in this collective desire which is expressed in 1789. And the nation – the National Assembly – regards it as part of its reforming role to deal with the clergy and ecclesiastical discipline, both of which leave much to be desired; moreover, the king himself will accept the Civil Constitution of the Clergy. One can see that the mention of the Supreme Being, which first occurs in the preamble of the Declaration of 26 August 1789, means that the compilers wish to make a break with Christianity and particularly with the Roman Catholic Church; for the Roman Church, this fact is even more significant than the freedom of conscience allowed by the Declaration. It is the Supreme Being who is superimposed on the God of Jesus Christ and his Church, placed above them both; they want to judge this Church in the name of the Supreme Being.

– The Terror is really a new Inquisition, isn't it?

– Yes, all governments by terror, all inquisitions, are a sort of inevitable outcome of the belief that one is the instrument of God or of a regime aimed at dispelling error and eliminating heretics and purifying a corrupt world.

– Where does the Declaration of the Rights of Man and Citizen fit into all this?

– If the Declaration extends beyond the French nation and shows itself to be universal in scope, is it not precisely because those who met in the National Assembly in July-August 1789 were all alike inspired with an immense desire to change the world, to transform humanity? These men, while making their autonomous declaration of rights, wished in fact to address the whole human condition. Most of them are Catholics at least by tradition; but they want to declare their rights and safeguard them legally, outside the domain of the Catholic Church – or indeed any Church.

– Should we think of the Church as having failed to keep up with the times?

– We must recognise the fact that the Church did not inspire these men's decision; the Church did not take the floor – which was more important than the taking of the Bastille. One can give a historical explanation, which is that the Catholic Church, with its hierarchical framework and its 'vertical' power-structure, was not at all used to paying heed to a 'horizontal' movement, coming from the people.

– I expect you know the definition of a Freemason: 'A free Mason in a free lodge'. Similarly, one could say of the Declaration that it affirms free human beings in a free society, each person having equal value and equal rights.

– But who exactly is this person?

– Basically, an adult male, a most rational man, who owns property and is his own master, a somewhat ideal, utopian man.

– You're joking, of course?

– No, not at all, I stress that the Declaration places great confidence in man and that the men who wrote it had an exalted idea, justified to my mind, of their own rational ability.

– A Christian cannot but be glad to see these men daring to take their destiny in hand in this way and looking forward to the coming of an ideal humanity. Of course the vision did not quite materialize but it was a step forward all the same.

– That was because of the immense difficulty, which these men of 1789 failed to recognize, of reaching a universal agreement on what it means to be human. But that in no way detracts from their merits.

The nineteenth century

   – Isn't it best to continue this line of historical inquiry?
   – We have seen the condemnation pronounced by Pius VI, as from March 1791. In 1832, Gregory XVI condemns Lamennais in much the same vein. Lamennais – this is before 1830 – denounces 'the alliance of throne and altar' and seeks, along with liberal Catholics, to reconcile the faith with a liberal position. 'The Church', says Lamennais, 'cannot preach religious, educational and personal freedom, and freedom of ownership and at the same time dissociate itself from those who are working for freedom on all fronts, and first of all, for freedom of the press.' The pope attacks this idea of the equal value of all opinions – what he calls 'indifferentism'; he believes that this leads to the 'madness' of thinking 'that absolutely everyone should be granted total freedom of conscience'. This, says the pope, can lead to 'nothing but trouble in the realm of religion and in society as a whole.' So the Declaration of 1789 is considered as disastrous for society as a whole and not only for religion: at the heart of this Declaration there are 'doctrines' which endanger the political power itself because these 'doctrines' undermine the loyalty and submission due to princes and sow seeds of dissent on every side. Thus Gregory XVI reverts to the idea of two powers, the spiritual and the

temporal; these are rival powers yet they exercise a joint responsibility for the welfare of the nation: anything that threatens religion also threatens the state; whatever threatens the state also threatens religion; this is of prime importance to governments of any kind, because their first responsibility is the maintenance of order and the fight against subversion of any sort. In similar vein, in 1863 Pius XI condemned the Polish uprising against the Tsar and ordered the clergy to submit to legitimate authority.

– If I may say so, I find this obsession with vertical obedience and this reverence for authority really amazing. It seems that the Church's teaching on human nature is constantly moving between two extremes, to both of which it is committed: the freedom God really did give to humanity, and the sin of humanity; a human being is at once free and a sinner; certain theologians insist that freedom is to be trusted, others are wary of it.

– Yes, but Catholics like Chateaubriand defend freedom; in the preface to the new edition of his *Essays on Revolutions* of 1826, he writes, 'I will not become an unbeliever again until it has been proved to me that Christianity is incompatible with freedom; then I will cease to regard as true a religion which opposes the dignity of humankind.' But it seems that the Church, when it speaks of freedom is thinking more of its own freedom than that of humankind.

There is a terrible saying, attributed to Louis Veuillot, which illustrates this ambiguity very well. Louis Veuillot is an ardent defender of Rome and says to the champions of 1789, 'When we are in the minority, we demand freedom in the name of your principles; when we are in the majority, we refuse it to you in the name of ours.' In an encyclical on *Freedom,* in 1888, Leo XIII states that the Church is not opposed to freedom; in fact, it has a precise conception of freedom – and the pope describes this conception in all its aspects in order to demonstrate the inadequacy of the liberal conception of freedom. So, all through the nineteenth century, the Church remains firmly opposed to the freedom demanded in 1789 but takes an opportunist stand, for example in the colonial affairs of the nineteenth century, to defend the interests of Catholic missions – then the Church argues in favour of freedom to promote all religious denominations, Catholic, Protestant...

– But was it only the Church which was opposed to the ideas of 1789?

– The 1789 Declaration immediately aroused violent opposition in several quarters. As early as 1790, Edmund Burke published his book *Reflections on the Revolution in France*. Burke is a forthright man, much attached to the English ideal of freedom; for him, 1789 has nothing to do with the English Revolution of 1688 and he utterly condemns 1789 as a revolution which he considers depraved both in principle and in practice, thoroughly evil in fact. In his eyes, the rights of man and citizen are the outcome of mere abstraction, a metaphysical system which is totally ignorant of the complexity of human affairs; these 'rights' are destructive because they tend to corrupt behaviour, dehumanise those in power and divide society. This conservative attack on an abstract equality which destroys both continuity and diversity will be renewed at intervals up to the present day by conservatives like Joseph de Maistre, de Bonald and others. On the other side, those who are called 'liberals' will attempt, throughout the nineteenth and twentieth centuries, to sort the wheat from the tares on the whole revolutionary scene and they will not utterly condemn the Declaration of 1789. For the liberals, a human being is not a creature with rights but with needs, and society is founded on the principle of exchange; Solzhenitsyn has several times made the point that liberals show a certain indifference to humanity, with their great emphasis on utilitarian principles. The champions of social

Catholicism, like Montalembert for example, react strongly against the concept of the private individual and so oppose human rights. But we should not forget another great opponent of 1789, in the second half of the nineteenth century: Marx; he strongly deplored the division of natural rights from civil rights – for him, civil liberty is a luxury reserved for proprietors; he is not interested in the juridical liberation of humanity but proposes the social emancipation of the masses.

– So the Declaration of 1789 aroused all sorts of very varied opposition: conservatives, Marxists, liberals and the Church. And on the historical level one has to agree with Hannah Arendt in her book *Imperialism* (Paris 1982) that in the nineteenth century, in the European nation-states, human rights were only more or less respected with regard to the general population of each state but were not guaranteed for those individuals outside their jurisdiction. Human rights were created for humankind, the group, the human race, not for the individual subject. But I'd like you to come back to Montalembert. When confronted with the economic and social problems of the nineteenth century, doesn't the Church speak very much in the same vein as the promoters of human rights?

– The answer is yes, but only partly so. In 1839 for example, the same Pope Gregory XVI forbids the slave trade and the recruitment of new slaves; he does not condemn slavery outright but seeks to bring about its gradual decline; the Protestants had long since preceded Rome in this area. But what is interesting is that, in this text, Gregory XVI speaks of the rights of all human beings, inveighing against 'this inhuman traffic by which blacks are bought and sold as if they were not human beings but merely brute beasts, reduced to a bestial level of servitude which is against all justice and humanity'. Leo XIII will repeat these sentiments fifty years later in the struggle against the slave trade in

Africa; and his Secretary of State will say that this struggle is not only in the service of the Christian religion but is also a highly social and civilizing move in the defence of human dignity which is so barbarously trodden underfoot by so many human beings.

As for the encyclical *Rerum Novarum* of 1891, we can find in this a real recognition of 'social rights', the right to work, to a fair wage, the right to form trade unions; such recognition is made in the name of natural rights. But Leo XIII in no way revokes the solemn condemnation pronounced by Pius IX in his encyclical *Quanta Cura* (1864) and above all in the *Syllabus* which accompanies it and is a catalogue exposing 'the principal errors of our time'. Among these errors is this: 'Each person is free to embrace and profess the religion which seems good to them by the light of reason.' And in 1906 Pius X will violently condemn the separation of Church and State and all those who wish to reach a compromise between affairs temporal and spiritual.

– Yet Leo XIII invited French Catholics to rally to the Republic in 1893.

– We must remember that the Church invariably pursues one primary goal: to construct a Christian society. And human rights are acceptable insofar as they are compatible with the building of such a Christian society. Leo XIII, much more of a diplomat than his predecessor Pius IX, seeks, as we have seen, to demonstrate the superiority of the Christian understanding of freedom (he calls it 'the most wonderful of God's gifts'); so he accepts civil liberties if they are in keeping with religion: 'Liberty means being helped by civil law to follow the prescriptions of eternal law more easily.' In this sense, Rome supports universal suffrage believing that divine authority can be mediated by human authority, elected by popular vote; in the same way, secular regimes may be acceptable if they do not explicitly reject God and work for the common good.

Human rights in our century

– But what do the nations themselves have to say about all this? I believe religious freedom is mentioned in the Treaty of Versailles.

– President Wilson, who was the real inspiration behind the Treaty, wanted the international community to adopt the system of tolerance in existence in the United States. There was a proposed article guaranteeing religious freedom; it was rejected by the sovereign states, and the only item retained were the accompanying clauses establishing the rights of individuals in minority groups; and freedom of worship is mentioned among those rights. It was a cautious step forward. Just before the Second World War, religious freedom is still regarded as a matter for individual conscience. President Roosevelt takes an important step in his 'declaration of the four freedoms' on 6 January 1941, in which he lays down the conditions required for future peace – the United States of America was not yet at war at the time. These four basic freedoms are: freedom of speech, freedom of worship, freedom from want and freedom from fear. This programme is incorporated into the United Nations Declaration of 1 January 1942. We are already on the way to the Universal Declaration of the

Rights of Man of 1948, which will declare in its preamble that religious freedom is 'inherent' in human nature; from then on, religious freedom is not considered as a mere concession made by governments but is seen as an objective value which is binding on them. Article 18 of the Universal Declaration of 1948 states, 'Every person has a right to freedom of opinion, of conscience and of worship; this right implies the freedom to change one's religion or convictions as well as the freedom to give expression to one's religion or convictions alone or in common, publicly or privately, by means of teaching, practice, worship and the performance of rites.'

– And what position did the Church take at that time?

– The body politic and the Church adopt somewhat different viewpoints here. We have just seen how, in the eyes of the various nations, freedom of religious expression had come to be linked with the concept of basic human rights. The Church approaches the question from a different standpoint; in the name of the common good, it assumes the obligation to create the necessary conditions for 'perfecting the human person', as Leo XIII and Pius XII put it; this means that the Church must guarantee to individuals freedom to practise the true faith. From Leo XIII to Pius XII, religious freedom is, in the eyes of the Church, a sort of positive civil right, a concession of authority; religious freedom is not justified by rights inherent to the human person. The popes repeat that 'it is contrary to reason that the true and the false should be accorded equal rights' (Leo XIII, *Libertas*, 1888) but they accept that 'in view of the common good', 'human laws may tolerate evil'. But the demands made of the Catholic remain unchanged. *Instaurare omnia in Christo*, as Pius X's motto has it, is the fundamental aim. So, without Christ, one cannot really establish human rights, as Pius IX says in *Quanta Cura*: 'Where religion is banished from civilian life, and the teaching and authority of Revelation rejected, the true concept of justice and human rights tend to become obscured and is lost.' In 1937 Pius XI will speak of 'Christian civilization' as 'the only truly human city'.

– At the same time, many Catholics in the French Church continue to reject 1789.

– A majority remain in opposition, forming a counter-Revolution opposed to both the liberalism 'unmindful of God's rights' and the socialism which 'rejects God's authority'. That is why, for example, in 1946 the Bonne Presse publishes a book with a preface by Archbishop Chollet on the *League of human rights*; the French bishops attack this League as a 'Masonic workshop' – the League was headed at that time by a Jewish philosopher, Victor Basch, who was to be murdered in 1944 with his wife by the Vichy troops; the book brings together all the counter-revolutionary arguments of a hundred and fifty years.

– And yet a layman like Ferdinand Buisson saw in the 1789 Declaration 'the translation of the Gospel into contemporary political language'.

– A small minority of Catholics will agree with this; Jacques Maritain is one of them.

– How does the Church react to the Universal Declaration of Human Rights of 10 December 1948?

– The Holy See makes no official comment. But two articles in *L'Osservatore Romano* deplore the absence of any religious basis in the text of the United Nations Organization; in fact Rome would have liked a preliminary article stating that human rights come from God. The article of 31 October 1948 in *L'Osservatore Romano*, before the Declaration was even published, is quite virulent in tone: 'As in 1789, it is human beings who legislate; they do not hold the Christian view, they do not accept anything outside themselves. They lay down the law. They decree according to their good pleasure what they will be able to change at will; and they will change, sooner or later, because by laying down the law in such a way they are making a fundamental error.' The French bishops remain silent.

The philosopher Jacques Maritain, one of those who contributed to the United Nations Organization text, will work with all his might to persuade the Holy See to recognise the Declaration of 1948. We will have to wait for John XXIII's 1962 encyclical *Pacem in Terris* to see a first move towards agreement. The encyclical starts by affirming the rights and duties which are 'universal, inviolable and sacred to every human being' (no. 9). But above all there is a key passage (nos. 143-144) which should be quoted: 'One of the most important achievements of the United Nations Organization has been the Universal Declaration of the Rights of Man... We consider this Declaration as a step towards the establishment of a juridico-political organization of the world community. This Declaration gives solemn recognition to the personal dignity of all human beings without exception and guarantees to each individual the right to seek truth freely, to follow a moral code, to act according to justice, to demand conditions in keeping with human dignity.' And John XXIII makes a firm move to heal the breach which had existed for two centuries between the Catholic world and the humanism of 1789 which no longer took God into account; a passage from *Gaudium et Spes* (no. 12) does not hesitate to state, 'According to the almost unanimous opinion of believers and unbelievers alike, all things on earth should be related to human beings as their centre and highest point.' 'Humanity today', says *Gaudium et Spes* again, 'is on the road to a more thorough development of the personality and to a growing discovery and vindication of personal rights.'

The breakthrough of Vatican II

– Yes, I know that *Gaudium et Spes* devotes a whole chapter to human rights.

– The revolution brought about by John XXIII and the Council arose from a new look at the position of human beings in society. On 17 September 1965 the English Cardinal Heenan will say that 'rights are to do with people, not things'; so we should not go on saying that truth has rights while error has none, but should rather speak of people and say that they should demand the right to seek freely for the truth; that is a basic right which should not have to be granted by the state, a right which belongs to all individuals at all times and in all places, whatever society they may live in. So all constraint should be removed, as well as all unreasonable fears.

Between the first two sessions of Vatican Council II there appears the encyclical *Pacem in Terris* (1962) in which John XXIII, as we have seen, makes a firm stand in favour of the exercise of modern freedoms. At the end of the Council there is a document which I would like to study with you now, called the *Declaration on Religious Freedom*, usually referred to by its opening words, *Dignitatis Humanae*. It is an extremely important document for our research on the Church and human rights.

– I imagine that it was not easy to agree on a text like that.

– There were certainly many difficulties in composing it. If we try to imagine the work that went into it, I belive it will throw much light on our subject.

– What is the main theme of this declaration?

– In this declaration the Council affirms without restriction the juridical equality of individuals in matters of religion; the Council defends the right of individuals to express their religious beliefs, that is, to practise quite freely whatever religion they profess.

– And what is the history of this declaration?

– There were six draft texts, with constant objections being raised and amendments of all sorts. The third draft, submitted to the bishops on 17 November 1964, meets with immediate opposition from the conservative wing; but it is proposed for general study; suggested corrections are sent in over a period of nine months; the fourth draft is the subject of heated debate in the Council chamber itself, so heated that the presidium wanted to postpone the vote; Pope Paul VI intervenes personally at this point and asks the assembly to answer 'yes' or 'no' to the possibility of retaining this fourth draft as a basis for the definitive text; the majority votes 'yes'. A fifth draft is then worked out and receives further amendments which lead to a sixth and definitive draft which is adopted by a vote on the last day of the Council, 7 December 1965.

– What were the fundamental differences of opinion, then, which led to such a lively debate?

– The Council had a body called the Theological Commission, led by Cardinal Ottaviani who was one of those who had composed the 1962 draft text on the Church which featured 'religious tolerance' and the 'relations between Church and State'. This text repeated the ideas of Leo XIII: God's sovereignty over human-kind is exercised in two different ways: the spiritual authority of the Church and the secular authority of the State; Church and State for Leo XIII are two autonomous communities but they need each other and should achieve their reciprocal aims in perfect concord. Working from this theory, the Theological Commission drew certain practical conclusions concerning the mutual duties of Church and State. So it argues that civil authority has a duty to give preference to the true religion, Catholicism. The Commission had as its political ideal the Catholic state in the manner of Franco's Spain. In an ideal state of this kind, if freedom of conscience is granted to all, including non-Catholics, the same does not apply to freedom of worship and teaching: the Theological Commission believes that the Catholic state can restrict the public worship of the non-Catholic faithful. Basically, the Commission takes up the position of Pius XII and believes it best for a Catholic state to oblige its non-Catholic citizens to practise their faith only in private.

– How on earth could they argue like that?

– They accepted freedom of conscience but held that a misguided conscience did not have the right to social freedom, that is, the freedom to profess and propagate one's faith in public; they took up Pius XII's principle: 'Something which fails to conform to the truth has no right to exist or to be taught and put into practice.' At best, a misguided conscience is only tolerated.

– But what happens in a state where the majority of the population is not Catholic?

– The non-Catholic authorities are still obliged to ensure the freedom of the Catholic Church and to grant all its citizens the right to live according to the Catholic faith. This is according to the principles of natural law which demand that 'civil freedom' be given to all faiths which are not contrary to this law. In a non-Catholic state, the Catholics must strive to obtain a decree of 'legal tolerance' which will enable the Church to fulfil its mission.

– Who was able to oppose Ottaviani's Theological Commission?

– Another body within the Church, the Secretariat for Christian Unity which obviously had a different viewpoint. One of its members, De Smedt, Bishop of Bruges, had stated clearly in 1963 that the Secretariat wished to move beyond the teaching of the nineteenth century; and he had said, 'Many non-Catholics are put off the Church, or at least suspect it of a certain Machiavellism, because it seems to them that we claim freedom of religious practice in a country where Catholics are in a minority, while we utterly refuse to grant the same religious freedom to others when Catholics are in the majority.' De Smedt wants to answer 'the question which the whole world is asking us: What does the Church think of the way in which religious freedom is most frequently defined and regulated in the heart of contemporary society?' Which means that the bishops were asked to stop speaking of religious freedom as a favour granted by the Church, and to regard it instead as an intrinsic reality of modern society, a reality about which the Church should state her opinion.

Seen like this, religious freedom is not only an inner conviction; it is a conviction freely exercised and practised, a freedom which is therefore an absence of constraint. Religious freedom is defined as 'a true right, based on the dignity of the human person' and this right means that 'in the practice of their religion, people should be free from coercion on the part of individuals or social groups or any human power'. The text of the declaration uses a double term: *liberi seu immunes*; it is a question of immunity; one is untouchable, if I may put it like that, when one practises one's faith; immunity is a precise term: if one invokes diplomatic immunity, for example, it is the privilege of a diplomat not to be subject to the jurisdiction of the state in which he resides. Where does the concept of religious immunity come from? From the dignity of the human person. And the first sentence of the Declaration on Religious Freedom immediately sets the tone of the rest of the text: 'A sense of the dignity of the human person has been impressing itself more and more deeply on the consciousness of contemporary humanity.' What is this human dignity? It means that a human being is endowed with reason and free will; so all should seek the truth and adhere to it only by free, personal choice. The text has some very beautiful lines on truth: 'The truth cannot impose itself except by virtue of its own truth and it makes its entrance into the mind at once quietly and with power.'

– So, in a way, we are back at 1789, which granted limited powers to both the authorities and the community, which may not take measures to prevent individuals from exercising their inalienable rights, among them that of religious freedom.

– I would like to stress the main theme of the Declaration: the dignity of the human person. The promotion and protection of human dignity should be among the basic aims of any society: everything should be judged from this standpoint, whether it be the internal affairs of a society or its international relations or the achievements of individuals striving to pursue their freely-chosen aims of justice, truth and goodness.

Paul VI will go to the United Nations in 1965 and will solemnly reaffirm his agreement with the 1948 Declaration; I often refer to a passage from his speech to the UN: 'What you are proclaiming here are basic human rights: dignity, freedom and above all religious freedom. We feel that you are giving expression to what is highest in human wisdom, we might almost say, its sacred character.' And on the twenty-fifth anniversary of the UN he will say, 'The Charter of the Rights of Man which your Assembly proclaimed more than twenty years ago, remains in our eyes one of its most glorious claims to fame.'

TEN REQUIREMENTS OF RELIGIOUS FREEDOM

Today the Holy See would like to present a paper on this subject, containing ten points. We would like to stress that the right to freedom of opinion, conscience, religion or conviction, implies the following freedoms:

1. For parents to pass on their own religious beliefs to their children, personally or with the help of the community.

2. For families to see their children's religious beliefs respected in all branches of education.

3. For every person to receive religious teaching individually or collectively or in their community.

4. For each community of believers to organize themselves according to their own hierarchical and institutional structure.

5. For each community of believers to select and train their future ministers of religion in their own institutes, to appoint them and subsequently transfer them, according to the objective needs of the faithful.

6. For each community of believers to open, erect or use buildings or places of worship according to the real needs of their members, with the assurance that buildings set aside for religious purposes will be respected as such.

7. For each community of believers to exchange news, to produce, acquire, receive, import and make free use of sacred books, publications and other religious material connected with the profession and practice of a religion or conviction.

– Let me try to sum up the ground we have covered so far: faced with this modern humanism without reference to God, the Church took fright and remained entrenched in its position. There seemed no way out of the situation. Vatican II opens negotiations again by

8. For each community of believers to have their own media of communication and to use them for religious purposes as well as having access to the various public means of social communications to the same end.

9. For individuals and communities of believers to have contact and common assemblies – including pilgrimages – with co-religionists in their own country and abroad; this to include the faithful as well as community leaders.

10. For every believer to enjoy effective equality with other citizens in all spheres of community life: economic, social and cultural, without fear of discrimination.

The delegation of the Holy See believes that these requirements represent the true desire of all the faithful. They hope that their conscientious search for the Absolute will be increasingly respected. They sincerely desire to be able to work without hindrance towards the civic, social and cultural advance of persons and groups in the society of which they are full members. They claim for their communities the autonomy and means necessary to fulfil their mission and witness to their faith.

In our opinion, these freedoms are fundamental: they also serve to enhance the co-operation and security, harmony and complementarity to which the peoples of Europe and of the world aspire, and for which we have come to Vienna.

Delegation of the Holy See
to the Vienna Conference (CSCE), 30 January 1987,
La Documentation Catholique, 1 March 1987

speaking of religious freedom as inherent in human nature itself, as an inalienable right which 'continues to exist even in those who do not live up to their obligation of seeking the truth and adhering to it'.

– Yes, and this is because the Council makes human beings and their dignity its central theme. Paul VI sums this up well in his speech at the close of the Council on 7 December 1965 when he speaks of 'human beings, as they really are, in our time', 'human beings who make themselves the centre of everything which concerns them'. Paul VI takes humanity as his starting-point, in the manner of the 1789 Declaration. So the problem is approached from the opposite direction.

– Does this represent a true reconciliation of the two kinds of humanism? Or is it simply a subtle adaptation of the nineteenth century pronouncements, without any fundamental change of principle?

– Even those who accuse Rome of being wedded to the *Syllabus* and refusing all discussion, even they are forced to admit that Vatican II has taken a new step forward here. And at the same time, the fact of proclaiming religious freedom and promoting it like this obliges the Church to move on from the position it still held fifty years ago.

– Is this an irreversible development? If Catholics came to be in the majority somewhere – supposing Poland became a 'catholic state' – would they go back to their former position?

– You seem to doubt the Church's conversion to the principle of human rights. Some Catholics certainly would like to move backwards and totally resume their former position. But the best thing for us is to take up the story from the end of the Council to the present day.

The Church and human rights since the Council

– In the seventies, the revelations concerning the Gulag Archipelago and what had taken place under Soviet-type regimes made people think very seriously about human rights. At the same time, there was a marked move towards *détente* and on 3 June 1972 the USA, the USSR, Great Britain and France signed an agreement on co-operation in Europe. US President Richard Nixon had just been to Moscow in May. Finland had meanwhile made an offer to all the European countries: she was ready to host a conference which would bring them all together. A long preparatory debate, at Helsinki, established four 'packages' of proposals on: security, co-operation in economics, science and technology and the environment, co-operation in humanitarian matters, and the follow-up of the Conference. The Holy See is invited to this Conference on Security and Co-operation in Europe (CSCE) and takes an active part, right from the preparatory meeting, in a discussion of human rights. Switzerland and Italy having made a joint proposal that respect for human rights be regarded as one of the essential foundations of international collaboration, the Holy See

A POSSIBLE DIALOGUE

Among basic human rights are freedom of opinion, conscience, religion or conviction. The Delegation of the Holy See noted with satisfaction the important place given to this topic by the various delegations. Practically every country was able to speak on the subject, express its point of view and justify its attitudes. This goes to show that in spite of the differences in the religious and agnostic – indeed even atheist – views of the world, it is possible to carry on a profoundly human dialogue, with mutual respect for each person's conscience. This is possible because we are people who inquire into and make statements about the whole human condition and nothing is more sacred than the sanctuary of conscience, which should never be subjected to constraint or external pressure. History abounds in proofs that repression and discrimination do not ennoble but rather diminish those who inflict them on others; a civilization cannot claim that name unless it can offer every individual the chance to develop not only on the material and scientific levels but also morally and spiritually. Believers hold that this sort of human progress, respecting the inviolable dignity of the person, stems above all from a certain openness to God.

Delegation of the Holy See
to the Vienna Conference (CSCE), 30 January 1987
La Documentation Catholique, 1 March 1987

asks that an explicit reference to religious freedom should be included. It is not a question of evaluating this or that religion but of insisting that the religious element is so inherent in human nature that political institutions cannot omit to mention it. Thus the Holy See puts forward two proposals: respect for religious freedom as 'essential in promoting friendly relations between the peoples of the member states'; 'the increase in the exchange of information of religious interest and the opportunity for individuals and religious organisations to make contact and meet for religious purposes.' Even the Soviet delegation agrees that religious freedom should be mentioned among the fundamental rights.

– It's interesting to note that not only has the international character of the Holy See been recognised, but also that the Holy See has taken up an ethical stand and returned to the theme of *Dignitatis Humanae*: in a pluralist society the individual's right to search for truth is a basic factor in social relations; so religious freedom should be in no way hindered by the public authorities.

– In October 1980, John Paul II sends a personal letter to all the heads of State who were signatories of the final Helsinki Agreement, in which he presents the problem of the place given by society to the demands of religion among the general needs of humanity; how, he asks, do we evaluate the relative importance of these needs? In November, Madrid sees the opening of a conference of all the members of the Helsinki Agreement; a meeting which will last until September 1983 and will be followed by others: Ottawa in 1985, Berne in 1986. The Western and non-aligned members maintain that all countries involved in the Helsinki Agreement should have the right to examine how the other member states are fulfilling their obligation; the Eastern bloc refuses to permit this.

– Throughout these talks, even if this last point is not agreed upon, no one questions that religious freedom is an inalienable right and that all its social consequences should be considered. At the Vienna conference (November 1986 – January 1989), the practical side is given closer attention. The final document states that no school or university candidates should be discriminated against on religious grounds and that communities of believers should be authorised to establish collective and individual contact both within and outside their national territory. In this way the Holy See wants 'religious freedom to be seen more and more as a civic and social freedom; so as to build a safer and friendlier Europe'.

– Isn't it a bit restrictive, this insistence on religious freedom only?

– At first, there were states which were a bit annoyed by this unilateral insistence on the recognition of religious freedom. But the argument that this freedom was a social matter and that a just and lasting peace within a country and between countries was impossible if religious faith and practice went unrecognised, was not without weight. Also of course this particular freedom must be compatible with the maintenance of public order and the common good. But that brings us into the area of mutual effort, on the part of the interested parties, to reach agreement by means of mediation and negotiation.

– Didn't the CSCE discuss religious freedom?

– The aim of the CSCE is a confrontation between the Western countries on the one hand, who set great store by human rights and consider civil and political rights as a constituent part of their cultural and juridical heritage, and on the other hand, the Eastern Europeans who stress economic and social rights rather than civil and political freedom. Until the Vienna meeting, the two blocs were at loggerheads; this situation eased up, partly because the East gradually began to adopt a different attitude to human rights. And we must remember especially the work that was done on the third 'package', the area of humanitarian concerns; the 'human dimension' of the CSCE is to be evaluated periodically so that human rights may become fully respected within the member countries. It is a very forward-looking project.

– Nor should we forget the work done at the United Nations during all these years.

– Yes, there is the Declaration on the elimination of all forms of intolerance and discrimination based on religion or conviction; this Declaration, adopted without a vote on 25 November 1981 by the 26th General Assembly, had been proposed in 1953; so it took twenty-eight years to come to fruition. Its preamble affirms 'the right to freedom of opinion, conscience, religion or conviction' and the eight points of the Declaration explain this right in detail. It was at the request of the USSR that the term 'conviction' was added in 1981 to include materialists, atheists or agnostic. At this point the United States delegate declared, 'In private or in public, each person's conscience is the source of their dignity, whether that conscience is religious or not.' Which statement was approved by the representative of the Holy See.

– That seems to me to present a problem. Should all religious minorities be accepted?

– In the course of the debates on the Declaration, the Austrian delegate asked, 'How can you put serious religions and sects on an equal footing? A credible Islam alongside excitable Shiites?'

The Declaration makes no distinction between recognised religions, sects and beliefs and gives preference to none. It is not concerned with the intrinsic value of the beliefs of these religious groups. But the Declaration does not permit these groups to participate in activities against the interests of either the state in which they live or other states; it is for the states themselves to judge as to the legality or otherwise of these groups. Thus the state is moved to intervene in certain cases when it considers the behaviour of a particular group to be damaging to public morals; on the other hand, certain sects, the Moonies for example, lead a so-called moral campaigning in opposition to secular pluralist institutions; other sects act as closed societies and serve as a cover for political activities on the extreme Right or extreme Left, bordering on terrorism.

– The sects are violently hostile towards the great religions but they are also quite often intolerant of each other; this sometimes takes the form of personal reprisals. But one could ask if the Roman Catholic Church doesn't behave like a sect at times?

– I was much struck by this passage from a Catholic philosopher, Jean-Luc Marion, 'If Catholics have become marginalised in modern society, it is because they have cut themselves off from modern thought. They have refused to think in the same terms as the rest of the world; which is actually the definition of a sect' (*New Observer*, 22 December 1988).

– The Declaration is a failure at this point: the member states who affirm religious freedom are not unanimous in affirming the right to change religion.

– Yes, they certainly backed down on that point, under pressure from the theocratic states; specific religious laws take precedence over basic universalist principles; each particular religion keeps to its own rules. And we must admit that this leads to a great loss of freedom in the many states where religious law predominates in this way.

– Shall we get back to the Roman Catholic Church?

– Let's talk about the pontificate of John Paul II with regard to human rights. A few weeks after his election, on 2 December 1978 John Paul II addressed the United Nations on the occasion of the thirtieth anniversary of the Declaration of the Rights of Man; in his speech he stressed, from the very first sentence, that 'human rights are clearly set out and taught in the Gospel message itself'.

– Yes, but there's a phrase John Paul II often repeats which bothers me a bit: 'Thanks to the Gospel, the Church possesses the truth about humanity.' In other words: the Church possesses the Gospel and therefore the truth.

– Well then, we should also quote this passage from the same speech of 2 December 1978: 'The human person, even when mistaken, always keeps an inherent dignity which may never be lost.'

– That is an answer but only a partial one. I know very well that John Paul II constantly reaffirms 'the equal dignity of all members of the human community' – as he does on the fortieth anniversary of the Universal Declaration, in 1988. But I would like you to dare to look, as a historian, at the way in which John Paul II's Church speaks about human rights. Some people say the Church is simply engaged in recovering its losses.

– Human rights, those of both 1789 and 1948, are based on a Kantian conception of autonomy. The dignity of which the pope speaks, on the other hand, is based on the biblical idea of the human person made in the image of God. If I may put it this way, the pope removes human rights and the dignity of the human person from the context of political theory and gives them a traditional 'Catholic' interpretation. For John Paul II, human rights have shown themselves to be wanting insofar as they have separated themselves from their religious roots; and the pope gives priority to religious freedom, not to freedom in itself; God's rights come before any other right.

– Was that the position of John XXIII?

– We should have to make a long analysis to answer that and we lack the necessary historical perspective. However, we can see the main lines of the picture. Without over-simplification, I think we can say that John XXIII and the Council saw the Church in the precise condition of a 'poor servant' vis-à-vis the world and in the world, a Church which has renounced its power, even its religious power, its privileges and political scheming, in order to be able to devote itself to its true task: the proclamation of the faith, and this in a very humble, ordinary way, without seeking to impose its views, putting its trust in humanity; thus the Church agreed to align itself with contemporary culture and at the same time sought spiritual renewal. There was no longer any question of a nostalgic longing for the temporal power it had lost a century earlier; and certainly no question of hurling anathemas at anyone.

The position of John Paul II is rather different from that of his predecessor Paul VI. Whether he is aware of it or not, the attitudes of this pope are influenced by the place the Church has always held in his native country. He wants a Church which assumes a position of supreme spiritual authority in the world, having the truth and the whole truth, an authority on ethics, able to declare the principles of a new universal order on the one hand and those of a new moral order on the other.

– Is John Paul II a political pope?

– Probably the most political pope of the twentieth century. He believes that the Church should be able to intervene endlessly on the political scene on account of its ability to solve ethical problems, on account of its very existence: it possesses and promotes the truth, so its political sense is bound to be superior to that of politicians. The world must be given a soul, it must be guided in the moral sphere; everyone, including atheists, should be presented with a comprehensible natural morality to which all may adhere.

– Shouldn't the pope make it quite clear how his authority is to be exercised with respect both to human rights and to those who think differently from him?

– And also the right time to exercise such authority. Now the pope tends constantly to dramatize the situation: he always represents the late twentieth century world as sadly misguided: reason is decadent, social relationships are in a state of ruin, society is in a kind of coma. So the Church and the papacy must hold out its best chance of salvation. He stresses the evils of modern life – for the pope, that means atheistic humanism, not to mention atheistic Communism: from the very start of the troubles in the East, the Church has been proclaiming loud and clear that Communism is extremely pernicious on account of being atheistic. Society has to be built on religion: when John Paul II declares, in his New Year message of 1988, that religious freedom is 'the foundation' and *raison d'être* of other freedoms, he is defending religious freedom and he has every right to do so, but he makes it quite clear that religion is a primary value in the modern world. This is the political theology of the Middle Ages all over again: laws and ethical values can have no authentic foundation except in religion. For the pope, defending human rights means defending religious freedom in such a way as to establish religion as the supreme value without which the human city cannot be constructed, and without which it is bound to collapse.

– You're not denying that there are forces of destruction, are you?

– When one sees the dangers threatening human beings today – I think, for instance, of the immense progress in the field of biology, with its advantages but also its risks – there is an urgent need to unite against the forces of destruction which exist today, forces which are more radical now than at any other time in human history. The Church should take part in this essential struggle on the part of humanity.

– Yes, but I fear that the Church wants to privilege the idea that it alone is capable of putting up an effective resistance to these forces of destruction. It's just another way of saying 'Outside the Church there is no salvation.' To insist on deducing human rights from the texts of Scripture seems like a kind of 'fundamentalism'; the Church proposes in this way to find a precise

A DEMANDING SORT OF SOLIDARITY

Human rights are the nucleus of a universalism still to be constructed... We need to base our solidarity with oppressed peoples not on our uneasy conscience, but on principles which we hold in common with them, we need to practise a demanding sort of solidarity, and therefore one that is conditional, a solidarity which seeks to avert a worsening of the situation. This means an internationalism which is not based on oppression, but which fights against oppression, not from a static position but from a position of progressively defined principles and concrete proposals which avoid alienating any party whatsoever.

Paul Thibaud, *Spirit*, September 1980, p.121-122

political programme in the Gospel; starting from these texts, it attempts to lay down norms and ethical principles for our time. John Paul II constantly refers to 'human beings, made in the image of God': he says for example, 'The deepest reason for the value and dignity of human beings, the meaning of their lives, lies in the fact that they are made in the image and likeness of God.' Yes, but this must be worked out in actual historical conditions; and the religion that makes this *a priori* statement must be able to prove, *a posteriori*, that it respects, not only the rights of God, but at the same time the rights of human beings and their dignity, freedom of conscience being one of their most important rights.

– In other words, Christianity has played a considerable part in the recognition of human rights; but the Church has not been sufficiently consistent in its practical application of human rights for one to be able to say that it alone was the originator of human rights.

– I'd like to go back to what we said on the subject of natural law. In the Middle Ages, it is universally taken for granted that 'nature' comes from God. St Thomas Aquinas is quite revolutionary when he advances a profane theory of natural law: natural law exists as such, even if there is no God; from then on, natural law seems to be a secular idea, based on reason rather than faith. John Paul II wants to go back to a natural law based strictly on faith. Reason is no longer thought to play a part. In a way, John Paul II reduces human freedom, and believes that this alone cannot be a basis for human rights. Secularism cannot be a value as such; it is the religious sense which should predominate and take first place.

– The Council recognised the dignity of the human person as the foundation for religious freedom. Here we have a natural law, rooted in human nature itself. The Council's declaration *Dignitatis Humanae* is the Catholic Church's true charter of human rights. During the discussions on this text the then Cardinal Wojtyla seems to have had real difficulty in admitting that a political law could be intrinsic in human rights; for him, human rights are a religious matter and come from on high and cannot be based on the complex secular process of history.

– We are always faced with the same problem; the difficulty that a religion like Catholicism has in recognising modern thought as such, in accepting the right of freedom of conscience, the right of subjective freedom. In fact, most religions find it hard to accept human beings' claims to autonomy in the face of God's law. But at the same time they find it very difficult to recognise that human rights do not originate purely and simply in a theological view of humanity; and that it is these very rights which have given rise to modern political society. John Paul II finds it hard to accept that if the Church is called to play a part in the debate on human rights and its practical application, it can only do so, in a democracy, as 'one among many' and not as a basic and central institution.

– In a secular society, religion plays a vital role, which is to ask endless questions, questions about the realisation of secular projects, questions about the lack of justice and solidarity.

– But there is much talk of the return of religion, of the 'fundamentalist' groups which seem to be seeking to take over in all religious faiths. These 'fundamentalists' want to refer everything strictly to religious revelation. This religious movement which arose some years back is highly critical of secular states with their tolerance and lack of censorship in the worlds of literature and drama; the Rushdie affair is an example of

Looking at the failures of history, the pope questions the value of contemporary ideologies which continually fail to observe and indeed violate human rights; His Holiness seeks to work out a new theory of those rights.

At the origin of creation, there is the Creator. According to the Catholic Magisterium, human rights are not to be considered except as being derivative from the primordial rights of God. Human rights arise from the duties of humankind to God, which are primordial and take precedence over any other rights. Here we are scarcely in accord with the modern declarations of human rights. The present pope sees in human rights the modernised version of the principles of natural law, which is the foundation of morality on a social, national and international level. The truly lawful state, then, would be one whose civil law was in conformity with natural law.

this; but if this affair is 'extremist' it is not unique. The tendency of religious faiths to pontificate and impose all their own values on society, is real enough; so we find an article in the Vatican newspaper, *L'Osservatore Romano*, dated 27 July 1988, attacking the Italian government, to whom it denies the right to campaign for the use of contraceptives in the fight against Aids; and what is more, there was the condemnation of Scorsese's film *The Last Temptation of Christ* without having seen it: 'The state should constantly recall its Christian foundations', declares Cardinal Ratzinger in his book *Church, Ecumenism and Politics* (St Paul Publications, Slough 1988). Here we have a radical questioning of the secular foundations of the state in favour of a 'Christian foundation'; which would lead the ecclesiastical au-

This constant reference to moral law, the law of God valid for all the nations, has given rise to much questioning, even condemnation. Some have seen it as an implicit questioning of the secular state as such, a turning away from the spirit of the Enlightenment... The Christian faith cannot accept the modern philosophy of secular morality insofar as this human-centred philosophy has either progressively marginalised it or eradicated it completely.

In the eyes of John Paul II, Europe has failed in its universal mission by denying its Christian roots and substituting a destructive secularism for a liberating Christianity.

J. B. D'Onorio, Director of the European Institute
of Church-State Relations, Speech of
1-2 December 1990: 'John Paul & Political Society'

thorities to decide, for example, on standards of moral behaviour.

– What is the secular realm if not that large space guaranteed by the state of law, a public area which is neutral and open where different elements of society may co-exist in peace, where all may express their convictions, whether these be humanist, moral or religious in nature? The modern state has no official religion or philosophy to offer but it has to know about all the convictions of its citizens; it must invite them to express themselves, to give their 'reasons' on important matters; it must be ready to recognise the contribution that this or that group makes to the nation as a whole. Sometimes people have laughed at tolerance; but it's a powerful idea; philosophers like Habermas show the efficacy and importance of 'communicative action', the necessity for continual dialogue between citizens, the continual need to reach a consensus, which cannot be achieved without mutual tolerance and rational deliberation.

A religion of human rights?

– The celebration of the bicentenary of 1789 has been described as a 'secular High Mass'.

– The chief of the Bicentenary Mission, Jean-Noël Jeanneney, was present at a discussion in March 1989 at the *Institute Catholique* in Paris on the subject of the revolutionary heritage in the Church; he expressed public regret at the 'extreme reticence' of the Catholic Church during this commemoration. And, in fact, the Church in France was hesitant about this commemoration, even when it could have concentrated its attention on human rights, which was precisely the main point of the anniversary (the *Declaration of the Rights of Man and Citizen*, 26 August 1789). And right at the end of this commemoration, many French people – including many Catholics – were astonished to see the episcopate refusing to take part in the homage given by the Republic to Abbé Grégoire at the Panthéon – Abbé Pierre, when questioned on television, said that he was 'sad and amused' by this refusal.

– And certain Catholics have shown a tendency, sometimes unilateral, to lay undue emphasis on the wars of the Vendée or on the martyrs, the Carmelites, for example.

– Not only Catholics. The historian Pierre Chaunu, who is a Protestant, has spent a large part of 1989 deploring the excesses of the Revolution; here is a passage from one of his articles (in *Liberalia*, 4, Winter 1989, entitled 'Justification for crime'): 'The Revolution', he says, 'unleashed the most severe religious persecution in our history. It strikes at any kind of religious belief and makes a mockery of its declared intentions of 26 August 1789... The anti-religious policy is responsible for the ghost of civil war which stalks our nineteenth and twentieth centuries. It led to the stunting of one of the most faithful groups of Christians who remained sadly mistrustful of the modern world. It discouraged them from taking their place in that modern world.' But many Catholics have tried to understand. Starting in January 1988, two Jesuits, Jean Weydert and Christian Mellon, organised a session on 'the heritage' of 1789.

– As for Archbishop Lefebvre's followers, they were delighted to denounce human rights; according to them, the Roman Church has allowed itself to be misled by the 'false teachings' of 1789, the source of all the trouble. There was also a Traditionalist reaction; starting in November 1988, there was a series of meetings at the Law Courts in Paris, under the direction of Pierre Daru, president of the Court of Appeal; magistrates and lawyers were invited to study what 'traditional' religion (*Figaro-Magazine*, 26 November 1988) had to say about human rights, 'the new religion of many of our contemporaries'. They reached the conclusion that human rights and God's rights are inseparable: both should be respected or both are thereby violated.

– You must have read an article by Jean Daniel which is relevant to our discussion, an article which appeared long before the bicentenary, in the review *Debate* of January 1987; it must have been a certain comfort to the Traditionalists: 'Human rights as a religion for unbelievers'.

– Yes, the article is most suggestive: 'The unbeliever', writes Jean Daniel, 'deprives himself of all means of coming to a knowledge of humanity by deciding to ignore its overwhelming religious dimension.' But he immediately goes on to say, 'If unbelievers have, for the last two centuries, been inclined to underestimate this dimension, we know that it has been in reaction to the Churches.' But how, then, is there any possibility of unbelievers having a religion? Can the unbeliever in his turn obtain some sort of religion based on the values of unbelief? Jean Daniel proposes a 'narrow way' which 'heads to a determined and forceful rehabilitation of a type of humanism which respects the divine without sacrificing to the gods'.

– The Traditionalists have not been the only ones to attack the human rights of 1789. I would like to quote an article by Jean-Marie Benoist, a philosopher and fervent Catholic: 'The Revolution against human rights?' If there is a question mark in the title it is because the author sees a double enigma in the situation: the Declaration of the Rights of Man is an enigma in itself; also, the fact that the Revolution 'should have set itself to flout, systematically' all the articles of the Declaration.

J.-M. Benoist acknowledges a real 'grandeur and nobility in the Declaration of Rights', especially on account of its 'leap' towards 'universality'. He stresses the importance of the first article: 'All men are born free and with equal rights'; the term 'equal rights', which is actually a direct borrowing from Rousseau's *Social Contract*, means that equality of rights which, in a secular and lay context, signify the respect for one's neighbour that is the manner and means whereby the law protects each person's dignity in a state of law. And J.-M. Benoist goes on to sing the praises of the law which 'acting as mediator in real-life situation, links us in relationship with others... Each person respects every other person, thanks to the juridical system, which makes me recognise the respect I owe to others because they are, like me, beings enjoying certain rights within a state of law.'

So it is not the Declaration in itself which Benoist questions, but the use made of it, from 1789 to the present day. For him, this Declaration was 'in its richness and simplicity, a weapon with which to fight oppression'; but at the same time people have used 'the forms of law to violate the law of nations', people have 'made a travesty of the right to judge by disposing of their countrymen under the pretext that they belong to a category now discarded and repudiated by history. And it is this cult of history, of Reason supplanting religion, that leads to the presumptuous ideology, the *hybris* of those individuals and revolutionary judges who dare to decide who will live and who must be eliminated.'

– Typically, Claude Lévi-Strauss reproaches the Declaration for its abstraction and sees that as the cause of all the trouble. Here is a passage from his book *From Near and Far* (written with Didier Eribon, published by Odile Jacob): 'The Revolution gave rise to ideas and values which fascinated Europe and then the world and gave France an exceptional prestige and influence for more than a century. However, one could ask if the catastrophes which have since befallen the West did not also arise from this source. People were given the idea that society was run according to the dictates of abstract thought when in fact it is based on habits and customs; by destroying these habits and customs in the name of Reason, one also destroys ways of life based on long tradition, and individuals are reduced to the condition of interchangeable and anonymous atoms. True liberty must be worked out in concrete situations.'

– In the same way, Benoist criticises 'the sort of thinking which seeks to solve the problem of happiness in the abstract and forces its conclusions on others, willy nilly', the thinking that 'is guilty of chopping society into segments and so reducing individuals, persons, to mere categories'. He sees a corrective for this abstract way of thinking. First of all, 'by an ethical system not based on a universally applicable law but on *people in individual, concrete situations*'. And also by reference to a transcendent Reality: 'Each one of us belongs to a humanity which is not only immanent and based on human nature defined by reason, but also mysteriously loved by God.' And Benoist refers here to John Paul II's encyclical *Redemptor Hominis*, published in 1979: 'Ethical demands', he says, 'are based on respect for individuals and love for persons, as the encyclical reminds us. Christ asks Peter, not only "Do you love?" but "Do you love me?" Here the transcendent mingles with the personal and the universal at the same time.'

– You have not spoken about this encyclical.

– That's true, you are right to remind me of it. All the more because this text is a real theology of human rights. We can find some striking views of the human person defined as 'the most important point in the visible world' because 'by his Incarnation, the Son of God *united himself in some way to each individual*' (my italics). So the Incarnation is given as the reason why humanity can and should be the unique and universal point of reference for everything: politics, economics, social life. Not only does John Paul II firmly support the work of the United Nations for human rights: 'The Church', says the pope, 'has no need to reaffirm how closely the promotion of human rights is linked with its mission to the contemporary world'; but he also links peace to human rights: 'Peace can be summed up as respect for inviolable human rights', and he declares that the act of violating human rights in peacetime 'is an incomprehensible struggle of human beings against their own kind'. The text is a sort of rediscovery of the theological foundations of human rights.

– I agree. But we shouldn't forget that this notion, based on the Incarnation, had already been strongly expressed, back in 1956, by the great Protestant theologian, Karl Barth, in his book *The Humanity of God* in which he says, 'From the moment that God became man, even the most wretched of human beings have had the right to protection from tyranny.' And this domestic legislation, if I may put it that way, should not lead the Church to place itself in the centre but should make it realise that the values for which it fights, for its own reason, are in fact identical with those which humanity has long since discovered and continues to discover daily, by the light of reason. You will remember what John Paul II said at Le Bourget on 1 May 1980 about the motto of the French Republic: 'Basically, those are Christian values.' Fortunately he added, 'I say that, being fully aware that those who first formulated this idea did so without reference to the covenant between humanity and eternal wisdom. But they wanted to act on behalf of humanity.'

– This phrase is perhaps ambiguous but interesting: the pope does not say that it is the Church – or Revelation – which gave rise to these principles; he recognises that those who *first* formulated them did so without direct reference to Christianity. His last sentence, 'But they wanted to act on behalf of humanity', indicates both that they did not act on God's behalf and that they did act with a view to helping humanity; but here, in work done for humanity, the centre of creation, John Paul II rediscovers the sense of Christ in humanity. We will return to these fundamental questions later on. I'd like to go on talking about the bicentenary and the reflections to which it gave rise, that are relevant to our theme.

– Yes, I found among the numerous articles dedicated to it, a sentence from Hegel: 'Robespierre is the man who took virtue really seriously.' Now this man, a devotee of Reason, wanted to carry out a kind of universal destruction of those who opposed what I might call the mystique of human rights.

– One of the books I found most interesting in the bicentenary year is one which is not exclusively about 1789. *The Conflict of Reason* by Manuel de Dieguez (Albin Michel) who considers 'rational thought' to be 'necessarily unbelieving'. In this essay, which is devoted mainly to the analysis of the phenomenon of religion, de Dieguez asks: 'What is the kind of rationality which inspires the lucid dreamers we call *prophets* who were able to base binding laws on the authority of celestial decisions?' The ninth chapter of the book is entitled 'Theology of the French Revolution'; according to the author, 'for two centuries, all historical meditation on the French Revolution has centred on the theological interpretations of the event'; in his eyes, 'the Revolution illustrates the very essence of Christianity.' I quote: 'The religion of human rights, which was born in 1789, is the Christology of the fifth century suddenly coming onto the political scene.' And what is 'the very incarnation of the Revolution and the Christian ideal together?' 'The Robespierre experience' which is 'the redemption of a nation which has become its own saviour.' 'Robespierre condenses into a few decisive words the ever-renewed history of Christianity.' He declared, 'Religion is the cohesive principle of society, the thing that prevents confusion between the destinies of the good and the wicked!'

– I must admit I've never seen Robespierre in that light before.

– De Dieguez's thesis is not without relevance: 'The evangelist of the people of Equality, called the Incorruptible', who 'understood that incorruptibility would be the new form of sanctity', starts as he says by 'espousing the cause of the people' and by defending the poorest of the poor at Arras; he is recognised there by 'the priests who are close to the common people'. Through Robespierre 'the real mainspring of the Revolution will be pure Christianity, which had been forgotten by the Catholic Church'. 'Robespierre's strength is to have understood that France was deeply rooted in a faith whose original meaning had been the sanctification of poverty. So the principle behind the entire Revolution would be Christian egalitarianism as preached by St Paul.' Robespierre gradually becomes the humble representative of the papacy of the people, the 'living commentary on the Declaration of Rights', as he himself says.

– Recent historians of the Revolution – Mona Ozouf, for example – have noted that the cult of the Supreme Being will coincide with a renewal of the Terror and that Robespierre wanted to link the Terror to a system of metaphysics.

– So de Dieguez quoted Bossuet: 'In the Scriptures there is a sacrifice which kills and a sacrifice which gives life,' and speaks of the 'religious foundations of the Terror'. 'It is a matter of employing a Cathartic purge in order to achieve a continual purification of society and ensuring, at the cost of bloodshed, that all humanity may give unconditional fidelity to the truths set forth in its catechism'. De Dieguez closes his chapter with a look at the 'worldwide history of Robespierrism'. 'Jacobinism, like the Inquisition, represents the passionate desire on the part of justice to rid history of evil by exterminating sinners.'

Respect for the individual

– There is a joint work which I would like to quote: *1989: Human Rights in Question Form* (French Documentation). Eli Wiesel, Emmanuel Levinas and thirty other thinkers discuss the development of human rights in a white paper which treats a number of questions, from religion to racism, from sociology to medical ethics.

– Another principal work on the bicentenary is the study of a Hungarian philosopher, Jakòs Kis, *Equal Dignity* (Editions du Seuil) with the subtitle *An essay on the foundations of human rights.* For Kis, those who are capable of debate on the basic principles of communal life are precisely those who qualify for equal human dignity. The study is preceded by an important preface by Paul Thibaud; he shows the origin of our democratic culture in the manner of Montaigne, for example, who believed that the city could be founded, not on commonly-held beliefs but on a *rapport* between individuals: 'If secularism has triumphed in Europe over the *cujus regio, hujus religio* (each country follows the religion of its ruler), it was because of its preference for interpersonal religion rather than the homogeneity of the community. So it is not by chance that Montaigne writes about friendship, "It is quite impossible to understand the whole adventure of modern Europe as a bringing together of people in relationship (of which human rights are one element), unless we first discern the foundation of friendship, the liking for human beings as human beings rather than merely members of my group".'

– Thus, for Kis, it is necessary to move towards some kind of universal moral authority, which presupposes the moral commitment of each person. We come back to the famous golden rule, universally valid: 'Do to others as you would like them to do to you' – a rule to be found in all cultures.

– More than ever, humanity today, plagued by its violence, divisions and conflicts, feels the need to seek some kind of communal moral structure; and human rights seemed to provide this supreme point of reference in whose light one would be able to evaluate a new law, condemn a police practice or the aggression of one state towards another; in the almost unanimous position of the United Nations with regard to Iraq, do we not see a living example of universal morality at work? It is a morality that is often disregarded but which is nevertheless accepted in principle by all sides; it is a morality which takes account of our world, where human beings are weak and oppressed, but can still refuse to accept the 'unacceptable'.

– That's the paradox of these last decades: the very strong appeal to respect the dignity of each human person and at the same time the reality of a lack of respect for so many human beings. One gets the feeling that humanity is moving forward on a knife-edge. Even a democratic system is not completely free from aberrations: a majority elected by popular vote can endanger human rights; Hannah Arendt has often spoken of this wretched side of human beings, these misplaced pretensions to identity and absolute uniqueness which go by the names of anarchism or nationalism, unsociability or egotism. The work of growing in awareness is never done: it is not the same as for scientific triumphs; moral imperatives must be won over and over again.

– In the future, even more than now, each person will have great freedom to lead their own life; thus there will be the danger of individual cynicism, but also the extraordinary adventure of the true liberation of each person.

– In his book on *The Defeat of Thought* (Gallimard, 1988), Alain Finkielkraut sounds a warning note: the modern world, dominated as it is by the relative and the particular, is suffering from a 'dearth of universality'. We must repeat the universal claim which is older than all philosophical or juridical systems: all human beings, in all ages and lands, have always needed and hoped for their rights, that is, to be treated in a certain way just because they *are* human beings. It would be a good idea to read the great volume published by Jeanne Hersch for UNESCO, which has such a wonderful title, *The Right to be a Human Being*, where this claim is shown to be truly universal.

– To what do we 'owe' this right? Is it because human beings are superior to the rest of the universe, being more intelligent than all other living beings and so able to command all things and yet be 'commanded' by no one?

– The right to be considered as an end rather than a means, as a person rather than a commodity, shows the sort of goal for which the whole human community should be ceaselessly striving: to build a sane world where each human being is respected in their own right and can live with dignity. Which means that we should not be preoccupied only with the immediate present and should never lose sight of our goal.

But I would like to go back to the definition of humankind based on its supremacy. I don't want to

HUMAN RIGHTS AS A FOUNDATION
FOR POLITICS

Human rights are not a matter of policy but the very foundation of politics. In the present day, there is no other political principle than the rights of the individual and the means of achieving them: that is, the right of each individual to develop to full capacity, to realise their potential and to be fulfilled.

The consideration of individual rights reminds us of the need to organise society in such a way that they may be put into practice. When we take human rights seriously, this suggests some kind of social ideal. But this ideal is different in form and nature from those suggested by the theories of class struggle. It is no longer a question of imagining a society where social opposition will have been overcome, but a society which is moving towards the goal of human rights for all. To relinquish the dream of harmony does not mean a free-for-all where the weak go to the wall, as long as it remains a common ideal, a desire to make different rights (such as those of liberty and equality) as compatible as possible with the rights of different individuals. The vital political question becomes the one asked by Diderot: What do we owe to one another?

Paul Thibaud, *Nouvel Observateur*, 1 January 1990

depreciate human beings, but is it really to their advantage if we regard them merely as superior in nature and power? I'm not at all sure about that.

– What exactly are you driving at? You know what Spinoza says about 'the joy that comes from the fact that human beings are powerful and capable of self-knowledge'. When we see that human rights are increasingly recognised – alas, I don't say 'respected'! – can't we rejoice to see how human beings consider themselves unique and how the majority wish to make human dignity the heart of their common life?

– Agreed, but I think there is something else. Human rights cannot mean simply a lot of human beings placed together yet each claiming their rights in isolation, being as it were an idol to themselves. How do we avoid that snare?

WHAT WE OWE TO OUR DIGNITY

All human rights flow equally from the fundamental right to that inviolable solitude where our grandeur grows in secret, in silent dialogue with transcendent altruism. That is why our rights can be identified with our duties for they express precisely what we owe to ourselves, or rather to our dignity, that is, in the last analysis, to the Love in which we must lose ourselves in order to be fulfilled. We can aspire to nothing less than being able to satisfy, without hindrance, the demand for that total detachment from self which will enable us to give ourselves without reserve. That is why we can firmly demand that society should respect the solitude in which our personality can be built up and which is, for that very reason, the true source of the common good. Society simply must grant us the freedom to enjoy such solitude.

Maurice Zundel, *Cairo Review*, May 1945

– And what is your answer to that?

– I seek an answer both in my reason and in my faith.

– Could you start with reason?

– This famous dignity exists when a human being can stand tall and find respect and recognition. Yes, but then what? Beyond that, there is the joy of seeing and desiring and acting in such a way that others, too, may be able to stand tall – all others; and, beyond that, the even deeper joy of being a disarmed force, as if one were vulnerable; the joy of having power but not letting oneself be fascinated by one's power, being someone who can, with humanity and humour, relinquish one's supremacy.

– Wouldn't that undermine the whole idea of human rights?

– Not at all, the way I see it. Because those who can distance themselves from their own power will be able to resist the fascination of the forces of death when these threaten to strike; they will refuse to use the power of the group to which they belong or any group which presents itself as being superior. And they will fight all the more against all the types of domination which are unbearable and unacceptable.

– Do you want to insist on inner freedom and the struggle for freedom?

– Yes, human rights should be applied to freedom, not the freedom to do anything one likes but the freedom to distance oneself, to gain some perspective, to be clear-thinking enough not to do just anything. Those men and women who have worked specially for human rights in this century have shown, in the midst of their task, this capacity for, I was going to say, humility.

Talking of which, I was struck by one theme which runs all through de Dieguez's book on Reason: the theme of the 'void', the 'desert', 'from which the spirit rises to discover itself grappling with its elusive identity', the theme of the 'meditation on nothingness'. Mystics like Meister Eckhart have dealt with this same theme. De Dieguez speaks of those who constructed systems of thought, 'general engineers of knowledge', and contrasts them with another 'race of intellectuals',

Socrates, Buddha, Confucius, Jesus: 'They say that reason burns up the idols which are always eager to occupy the night of transcendental thought.' Reason 'stands aside humbly to give place to silence; reason destroys illusion, so that the spirit can become truly alert'. This confrontation with the abyss is the opposite approach to the one which seeks to make everything smooth and workable. One can turn human rights into a vague, watered-down ideology full of noble sentiments while forgetting the continued existence of inhumanity, getting out of this difficulty in Manichaean fashion by attributing evil to some 'other' and living under a naive illusion of harmony by treating all values as equal. In reality, we should be going forward, using our reason to the full, without relying on false reasoning, not allowing ourselves to become intoxicated by our own power and majesty, not making little tin gods of ourselves, which would actually make us lose our freedom. And it is here that we are in agreement with Levinas and his insistence on 'the rights of the other person', on the generosity, the liberality with which I go out of myself and towards others, going beyond myself to meet their needs: 'One can ask oneself', says Levinas, 'if clothing the naked and feeding the hungry is not the true and concrete way of discovering their otherness.'

The other person's rights

– You're going a bit fast, here, suddenly talking of the 'other person's rights'. I know the charter of 'the other person's rights' composed by the Human Rights and Solidarity association and you told me that they had received letters of complaint about this charter.

– Yes, and it is precisely in this way, I fear, that 'human rights' can become watered down; when one thinks of 'human rights' solely in terms of individual survival or the defence of a thousand little egotistical rights – there was talk of a 'right to be idle', for example; is that really a 'human right'? The right to differ has often been used to justify my more comfortable life-style; so misery and death have been brushed aside as unimportant, something which happens to others. It is difficult to speak of the 'rights of the other person' because it immediately faces us with the fact that other people, strangers, who, as Segalen said, are 'radically incomprehensible', have a right to exist just as they are, the right not to be made like me. 'To proceed according to reason' is above all to maintain this sense of the other's inviolable 'otherness'.

We should not let human rights lead us to a sort of grand illusion, a universal pantheism with us all singing songs of togetherness in an atmosphere of synthetic peace and goodwill.

– Besides, if I lose the sense of the irreducible otherness of the other, I can no longer give to them or receive from them; there is no longer any real communication.

– Other people's rights show me that I must at the same time be true to myself and also make a true relinquishment of my desire to dominate and my ready tendency to totalitarian views – which turn me in on myself, profitlessly. Perhaps we should make it clear that if you have a true regard for the rights of others, you open yourself to the possibility of receiving a great deal from others as well as giving something to them.

– And from the point of view of faith?

– My faith shows me Jesus and the commandment of charity, of love, that is, something other than strict reciprocity – the rights and reciprocal duties of each person which are implied by human rights. True love goes beyond this: one doesn't love someone for some ulterior motive or because one is obliged to do so; love goes beyond such reasons; it is gratuitous, generous, inventive; it means a spontaneous movement towards the other person. One very important factor in human dignity is the ability to give oneself, for only a free being can do this, someone who is one's own person, a being who can appreciate human values and apply them for the benefit of all human beings.

Rights can so easily be restricted to purely material and quantitative claims; love, and therefore all true faith, is there to urge human rights onward in imaginative ways, leading to true solidarity. At the same time, human rights, which are a matter of justice, are a real challenge to charity, which can never operate in the same way. Charity and justice should never be confused but should each act upon the other.

CHARTER OF THE RIGHTS OF OTHERS

Here and all over the world
The other person
The one who is not in my group or does not share
    my opinions, the one who is not the same age
    as me or does not share my life-style,
the one who does not come from my district or
    from my country, race or skin colour,
the other, each human being, whoever it may be,
    has a right to life and happiness,
to space and freedom;
each human being has the right to an equal
    dignity.

Because other people are unique
Their history and destiny are unique;
in the midst of all the others, subject to laws and
    duties like all others,
they are unique persons
who have the right to be recognised for
    themselves,
they have the right to their own faces, their own
    way of speech,
they have the right to respect for their identity,

they have the right to work, to develop their
    abilities,
they have the right to love and to celebrate,
they have the right to belong, the right to the
    culture and community of their choice,
they have the right to come and go freely through
    the whole wide world,
they have the right to peace.

The other person is worth the trouble
Each human being who is not respected in their
    own right,
each human being who is used, manipulated or
    despised,
each human being who is silenced or starved,
each human being who is prevented from acting
    for their own good or the good of others,
each human being who is hounded or oppressed,
    locked up or rejected
has the right to receive from me,
here and now,
the real help of my thoughts,
of my heart and of my hands.

Human Rights and Solidarity

The Church needs to sweep its own front porch

– Let's get back to the Catholic Church and human rights.

– We have read the history of human rights and we've seen that even if they have doctrinal roots in Judaeo-Christian ethos, they have developed outside the Church and have for a long time found a determined enemy in the Church praxis. Today, when human rights are held in honour by the Catholic Church and taught by its Magisterium, we must be quite clear: the Magisterium should avoid any kind of authoritative monopolization of these rights – and the temptation to do so today in the area of ethics is great; of course, the Church may and should speak out; it should do so by stating quite clearly its own doctrinal reasons for embracing human rights; but the Church is not the one and only foundation of human rights; there are other authentic religious families, other schools of spirituality and philosophy which have also contributed to the development of human rights.

The Church should remain humble; as far as it is concerned, the one foundation for human rights is the Word of God revealed in Jesus Christ; now the Church has failed in some ways and sometimes deeply betrayed human rights in the course of history.

– Has the Church admitted to these errors?

– I would like to quote here what Jean Delumeau wrote in *A Guide to Theological Development 1990-1991*; this historian, having proudly examined Christianity's contribution to history, wants to take a clear, dispassionate look at the less praiseworthy moments of Church history: 'While being grateful for a rich contribution in the past, we must admit our mistakes quite frankly in order not to repeat them. Now there is still too much ambiguity in the official language of the Catholic Church. For example: nowadays human rights are held in honour but we forget that Pius VI condemned the Declaration of 1789. It is an excellent thing to exalt human rights but we need to declare all the previous condemnations null and void! If we don't do that, we are quite simply engaged in 'double-talk'. And even today one can understand that some people should have reservations on the subject. This is what Fr Reynaert has to say in *Liberation* (9 February 1990): 'As for John Paul II's much vaunted spirit of tolerance, this "eternal pilgrim for human rights", as television reports call him, one could be a bit doubtful about that when one hears him say things like this: "The only civilization worthy of humanity should be Christian".' And the assessment made in the joint work *The World of 1989* (Discovery Publications) is disturbing for any Christian who is a bit too rigid in these views, or averse to publicity. I am reminding you of all this, not that we should get caught up in quite fruitless condemnations, but in order to encourage true vigilance, and above all in order to have as clear a picture of the situation as possible.

And the Church absolutely must make a close examination of modern humanity, the humanity which gave rise to human rights and the democratic society: the society which claims the right to exercise its own moral conscience, whose members are free beings, both reasonable and responsible. Modern society has become profoundly allergic to obedience in any form; it rejects external authority, as also the concept of a transcendent, law-giving God; and it hates to be told exactly how all human beings should behave. Don't let us immediately assume that such a society wants to 'do its own thing' exclusively or have unlimited freedom; no, this society – and why not trust it a bit? – is looking for a responsible sort of freedom, based on enlightened reasoning. And this society seeks at the same time to respect the personal conscience of each member, to respect all free persons in their struggle for greater freedom and to enter into dialogue with them.

For a Christian, freedom of conscience can be perfectly well combined with that other spiritual movement which is faith, the acceptance of the 'other', the God of Jesus Christ. But it is still necessary for the Church to pay close attention to the way modern humanity is going and it should have a deep respect for the ways and means by which modern society seeks to advance, freely, towards faith in the God of Jesus Christ, a faith which does not involve abdication of one's intelligence or humanity.

– Yes, if the Church is to speak of human rights, it should first sweep its own front porch and satisfy the demands of its doctrine of human rights within its own organisation; this should lead it to correct the abuses in its own life.

– Can you be more explicit?

– Yes, I'll do so by quoting a short article published by a Spanish theologian, José Marina Diez-Alegria, in a joint work on *The Declaration of the Rights of Man of 1789 and its Repercussions on the Catholic Church* (published by the Institute of Faith and Secularity, Madrid 1989). The article in question is entitled 'The present position of human rights in the Church'. The author passes from human rights 'as preached by the Church to the demand for legal recognition of these rights inside the life of the Church itself'; using numerous examples, he points out the right, in the Church, of freedom to seek for the truth, freedom to 'work according to the just principle of individual conscience', freedom to express a sincere opinion publicly; he also mentions the right to autonomy on the part of intermediate social organisations, active participation in public life and the juridical safeguarding of human rights.

'In the Church,' writes Diez-Alegria, 'there is no declaration of human rights but only, in the new Code of Canon Law, a declaration of the duties and rights of all the faithful. This is a grave error because human rights should be in force in the Church and not only the rights of Christians by virtue of their baptism.'

The author stresses that it is 'essential' for the legal validity of the recognition of rights that there should be effective legal protection through impartial procedures, 'especially in the case of conflict with authority'.

In one of the early drafts of the Code of Canon Law, such administrative procedures had been provided for; but this provision was withdrawn from the final edition of the Code and those in the Church who feel their rights are not being respected can have no recourse to administrative channels other than their immediate ecclesiastical superior. One can see that this is a serious deficiency.

Diez-Alegria stresses another deficiency in the Catholic Church: the lack of respect for the 'subsidiarity' principle: 'The principle of centralisation continues to prevail over all attempts at decentralisation... The administrative and juridical system prevails over the theological; in the name of security, there is a tendency to quell or at least to restrict any kind of intervention on the part of lower-ranking members to the hierarchy.'

And there is, in the texts of canon law dealing with the ecumenical council, 'a basic lack of equality (with incredibly authoritarian overtones) between the primate and the College of Bishops. The pope is entirely free and unrestricted in his control over the activities of the council. There was a move by some members of the preparatory commission to define objective limits to such authoritarianism, but it was defeated.'

As for the process of nominating bishops, 'one would search in vain for any kind of guarantee of community participation or any restriction to the autocratic procedures involved.'

The procedures of the Congregation for the Doctrine of the Faith seems 'particularly scandalous' to the author: 'There is no separation between the authorities which make an accusation and those which judge it; the same authority does the research, brings the accusation and pronounces judgement.' And Diez-Alegria gives a blow-by-blow account of this procedure whereby the accused is left out of account.

The very way in which the new Code of Canon Law came into being, leads the author to this conclusion: 'The authoritarianism and regal absolutism which this shows is contrary to human rights and in my opinion there is absolutely no credal justification for such behaviour.'

– It will doubtless take an extensive struggle to modify these institutional customs in the Roman Church in the direction of freedom and respect for human rights.

– The consequences of such customs are serious – P. Huizing, a theologian, says: 'The impression that Catholics believe because the hierarchy tells them so, is so strong that it even diminishes the credibility of the Gospel in the eyes of Catholics themselves... The Magisterium is not a force for imposing or prescribing the faith; it operates solely in the midst of the living community and is rooted in the faith of the whole body of believers' (*Concilium*, 19, 1983).

– Father Christian Duquoc has recently brought up the question of democratic procedure in the internal administration of the Catholic Church: 'There is something pernicious in this rejection of democracy,' he writes. 'But the Church is well able to make its style of administration more democratic without jeopardizing its obedience to the Word' (*Woman, Priest and Layman*, Labor et Fides, 1989). By all means let there be some form of administration which will help to give structure to the various communities of the faithful; but its purpose should be to help all the baptised to fulfil their mission as witnesses to Christ in the world. A hierarchy does not exist for itself, outside time; one cannot be a bishop today with superb disregard for the democratic systems of modern society and the values introduced by these systems; a tolerant pluralism, a real sharing of responsibility, the possibility of dialogue. John Paul II declared at Seoul, in October 1989, that democracy is in complete conformity to human nature; why not apply the democratic spirit to the Church and establish a permanent dialogue between the lower ranks and those in authority?

– All the more because a democratic system would protect the ecclesiastical authorities from their constant temptation: clericalism, and would prevent them from abusing their power. But I think that there's a move towards democracy, for example, in the increasing number of diocesan synods: the Catholics of one diocese discuss and decide matters with their bishop.

– Better still, if human rights are seen to be observed in the very heart of the Church, it will be better able to preach human rights to the outside world and will be able to encourage others to apply these rights more widely and more efficiently.

– Human rights are everybody's business, an ideal

which must be lived out daily by all, individuals and institutions, Christians and followers of all religions and persuasions, a dynamic force which should draw us all together.

CHURCH, ECUMENISM & POLITICS

by Joseph Ratzinger

"The articles and papers collected here form a kind of second volume to the ecclesiological essays which I published in 1969 under the title *Das neue Volk Gottes*. The basic issues have remained the same: the question of the nature of the Church, its structure, the ecumenical scene, the relationship of the Church and the world. But in many cases the emphasis has shifted and new evaluations have become necessary.

The debate about Christian ecumenism and efforts to achieve the right relationship of faith and politics occupy the foreground of the reflections that make up this volume. Some of the contributions reprinted here aroused vigorous debate when they were first published, and I have tried to do justice to this debate either in additional footnotes or in newly added postscripts. I hope that in this way it will become clear that these essays are meant as a contribution to dialogue with the aim that by listening to each other we shall be able to hear more clearly Him who in His person is the word and truth."

278 pages   ISBN 085439 267 X   £9.95

LOVE IN THE ECONOMY

by Christopher McOustra

Love in the economy summarizes the last hundred years of Catholic teaching on the role of the individual in modern economy, covering topics such as housing and shared ownership, the "social mortgage", pay and profit, and the rights and responsibilities of men and women in business, at work and in Trade Unions. The Vatican Council, Popes and bishops repeatedly present a social doctrine based on Christian love. In the words of Pope John XXIII "love is the driving force of the economy" and the hallmark of the Christian social doctrine. The author, sifting through the main documents of the Church – from Pope Leo XIII's *Rerum Novarum* (1891) to Pope John Paul II's *Christifideles Laici* (1988) – identifies the specific character of the Church's teaching on social issues. An anthology and guide book for all Christians, especially priests and teachers, workers and students, members of Trade Unions and businessmen, who care for peace and progress in a society often motivated by sheer profit and power.

CHRISTOPHER McOUSTRA, *Master of Arts at Christ's College, Cambridge, trained as a lawyer, and from 1959 to 1982 worked in British Industry.*

222 pages   ISBN 085439 324 2   £7.95

WITH EYES TO SEE
Church and world in the third millennium

Walbert Bühlmann

Bühlmann offers a searching, perhaps controversial analysis of the Church and her mission in the world in the light of the teachings of Vatican II. "The worldwide world and the worldwide Church now call for a new world order." He insists that "Christians have the task of underpinning all of this from the Gospel which today calls for prophetic speech and action."

Three main themes run all through the book. The first is that of hope: in these difficult times, prophets will be sent to us to show us the way and lead our people out of exile. The second is about the tension between documents and deeds: we are drowning in documents all the while thirsting for deeds. The third theme: is Rome still simply going its traditional way?

Bühlmann concludes with a stringent call to action: "the Holy Spirit takes us all seriously... The hour of truth is striking. No longer can we point the finger of blame at the pinnacles of the Church. No longer do we ourselves get off scot-free. All criticism of the Church, all Church reforms, all hope for the Church, must begin with you and me. Nothing is hopeless so long as we ourselves do not collapse in hopelessness."

WALBERT BÜHLMANN, *born in 1916 at Luzern, joined the Capuchins and was ordained priest in 1942. He took a degree in theology at the University of Freibourg in 1949 and joined the Tanganiykan missions of the Order. From 1954 to 1970 he taught missiology at his alma mater. In 1971 he was appointed Secretary General of the Capuchin's' Missions. He lectured at both the Gregorian and the Urbanian Universities in Rome.*

176 pages   ISBN 085439 342 0   £7.95

THE HEALING POWER
OF PEACE AND NONVIOLENCE

Bernard Häring

Literature on peace and war has increased enormously in the past few years. Catholic, Protestant and Jewish scholars are filling bookshops with scientific and popular writing on this Number One topic, which people see as being nothing less than a question of 'to be or not to be'. Why, then, this book?

Fr Häring wants to open the horizon for the broader, underlying questions. No moral theologian or ethicist has, up to now, given systematic attention to a *therapeutic* approach, presenting a therapeutic spirituality and strategy. This is what the well-known Catholic moral theologian tries to do in this book, hoping that others will take up the theme and develop it.

Many theological and pastoral concerns flow together in this treatise. The fundamental element is a coherent, therapeutic understanding of redemption, reconciliation and liberation, as found in the best Christian tradition.

If humankind is in extreme danger of self-destruction then there is nothing more important than to join in the whole-hearted search for the saving truth and for effective remedies: 'How can we help the sick if we do not recognize what is sick in ourselves and have not learned to accept the others as sick people?'

This is one of Fr Häring's major studies. It works out a dimension of the peace-problem so far scarcely touched.

132 pages   ISBN 085439 244 0   £4.95